SOME ASSEMBLY REQUIRED

Mixed Technique Quilts

margie engel

AQS Publishing

Located in Paducah, Kentucky, the American Quilter's Society (AQS) is dedicated to promoting the accomplishments of today's quilters. Through its publications and events, AQS strives to honor today's quiltmakers and their work and to inspire future creativity and innovation in quiltmaking.

Executive Book Editor: Andi Milam Reynolds
Senior Editor: Linda Baxter Lasco
Graphic Design: Lynda Smith
Cover Design: Michael Buckingham
Quilt Photography: Charles R. Lynch
How-to Photography: John Engel

Additional copies of this book may be ordered from the American Quilter's Society, PO Box 3290, Paducah, KY 42002-3290, or online at www.AmericanQuilter.com.

Text ©2011, Author, Margie Engel
Artwork ©2011, American Quilter's Society

Library of Congress Cataloging-in-Publication Data

Engel, Margie.
 Some assembly required : mixed technique quilts / by Margie Engel.
  p. cm.
 ISBN 978-1-60460-008-7
1. Quilting--Patterns. 2. Patchwork--Patterns. I. Title.
TT835.E524 2011
746.46--dc23
                    2011030197

THANKS!

Sincere and Grateful Appreciation (accompanied by gigantic hugs):

To God, for our creative spirits and constant blessings.

To John Engel, still my best friend and photographer, for technical know-how, wise guidance, never-ending encouragement, and for still smiling about prevalent threads and fuzz-balls.

To my daughters—heartwarming individuals—for their enthusiasm, understanding, and assistance.

To my grandchildren, quiltmakers in their own right, for lighting up my life.

To Gene Ives, gracious friend and talented artist, for providing insight and treasured inspiration.

To the numerous students and guilds who welcomed my classes, for teaching me more than I taught them.

To Andi Reynolds, matchless executive editor, for genuine support and honesty.

To Linda Lasco, unbeatable senior editor for amazing efficiency, support, and superb scrutiny.

To the multitude of AQS folks who had a part in this book, for sharing their talents so beautifully.

ABOVE and OPPOSITE: This New Day, detail. Full quilt on page 36.
TITLE PAGE: Floral Reflections, detail. Full quilt on page 19.

WHAT! CONTENTS

'TA-DA! Moving Forward with Ideas

Magazines, books, television shows, quilt festivals! Who has not gazed at a quilt through one of these media, uttered an immediate "Wow!" and stopped for a second look? Then there is the third look as the quilt draws you closer for a lingering experience to admire its originality, its amazing execution, or its ability to simply inspire you.

What makes that happen? Usually, it is an emotional reaction to something about the quilt, and that something varies from person to person. It might be appealing colors, good design, gorgeous fabrics, a special personal attraction, or all of these combined in a way that speaks to the individual.

In your own quiltmaking, the quest for that special something is part of the healthy growth of a passionate quiltmaker who looks for new techniques, novel ideas, and perhaps even new embellishing concepts. While on that quest, it is nearly impossible to confine a quilt to one technique—pieced blocks get lonely and go in search of appliqués to give them completion; appliqués start looking for embellishments; and suddenly, you have a project on your hands resembling Joseph's coat of many colors! It is a quilt of many techniques in search of a good design.

What should one do when she decides to expand her repertoire but hesitates, feeling uncertain about the design? If that is you, begin by shrugging off the feeling that you cannot be a designer. Of course you can. If you have been quilting, you have been designing in one way or another—changing colors, selecting fabrics, or moving blocks around—so it is time to consciously move forward. Bravely take one foot out of traditional quilting. The worst that can happen is that you will learn a whole lot more than you knew before. Besides, you have another foot!

Okay, with one foot stepping into contemporary ideas, where do you begin? Perhaps with one of these:

- *an idea that has been bouncing around in your head*

- *a scrumptious piece of fabric that you have hesitated to cut*

- *a yearning to express a feeling or an emotional reaction to an event*

- *a photograph or mental image that appeals to you*

- *a memory that tugs at your heart*

- *a favorite quilt block (See? You can keep one foot in tradition!)*

Idea in head and fabric in hand, suddenly you encounter the first dilemma—how to get started. We've all heard the professorial answer—to begin at the beginning—but where is that beginning? For the sake of organization, let's begin with a basic design. Several are included in this book for you to use as springboards.

Me, a designer? Yikes! Yes, you. Go for it. Start with my samples, add some filler blocks, maybe some appliqué and embellishments, and follow your heart.

LEFT: Splash, detail. Full quilt on page 20.

Some Assembly Required • Margie Engel

You want your design to be a good one, so think about some of the necessary ingredients—balance, focus, color, and unity.

Begin with Balance

A good place to start is with our feet on the ground. That, after all, is what balance is all about—the feeling that you aren't falling off the world; the distribution of weight that relates the feeling that how much of something on the right is also on the left; or, visually, whatever is on the top is equal in importance or weight to what is on the bottom. It is simple, until someone tells you that there is formal balance and informal balance, symmetry and asymmetry. Look at figures 1–3 below. Each illustrates symmetry—balanced, unified, and comfortable.

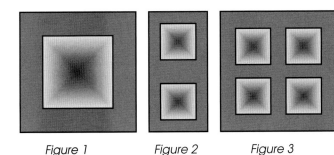

| Figure 1 | Figure 2 | Figure 3 |

For a moment, look at figure 3 and ask yourself if it can be improved by changing something to add interest.

Let's try moving two squares to improve eye appeal.

 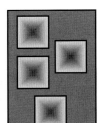 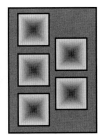

| Figure 4 | Figure 5 | Figure 6 |

Is figure 4 more interesting than figure 3? Is figure 5 more interesting than figure 4? Try comparing figures 4 and 5. If you find them more interesting than figures 1–3, then you are on your way to finding ways to add interest to your quilt plans.

Figure 5 definitely draws more attention, but a new challenge emerges with excessive negative (unfilled) space. One obvious solution is to fill the space with another block, as shown in figure 6.

Look what happened. The balance shifted from symmetrical to asymmetrical! Now, your job is to determine which type of balance brightens your day. Do you prefer symmetry or asymmetry?

Symmetrical and Asymmetrical Balance

Symmetry
Harmony that results from balanced, mirrored proportions and weight

Asymmetry
Balance achieved by variety but still yielding equal visual weight

Ready for the next question? Ask yourself, "How can I make this still more interesting?" How does one make something that is good even better? Many times, using odd numbers works.

One solution:
Change something. Try altering the size of one (or more) of the blocks.

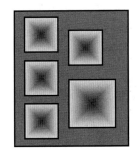

Figure 7

LEFT: Floral Reflections, detail. Full quilt on page 19.

Another solution: Change the shape of the blocks.

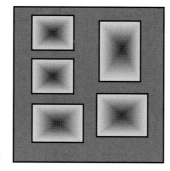

Figure 8

Something else happened in figure 7. Changing the size of the blocks made one block more important than the others. You have just incorporated another important design element—that of focus.

Balance
Exercise

A good way to develop your sense of asymmetrical balance is to cut paper shapes of various sizes and play with them by arranging them into different configurations. You can also do this on your computer if you enjoy drawing with software.

Factor in Focus
Success Factor:
Dominant features create excitement in quilts.

Next, think about focal points. Many quilters get so wrapped up in process, that they forget that a focal point is one of those important necessities of a contemporary quilt's impact. What is it? The attention-getter, that place to which the viewer's eye is drawn. Where the eye goes from there is up to you, the artist, but it has to start some place, and that place is the focal point. So, keep the main thing the main thing!

Then you ask, "Can I have more than one focal point?" Of course you can. This is your quilt. However, your viewer will still seek a starting point that dominates, a place upon which her eyes will come to rest.

Focal points are established in many ways:

By size: As shown in figure 7, making something bigger draws attention to that item, whether it is a quilt block, a motif, or a section of a collage.

By placement: For interest, place focal points off-center; off-center does not have to mean over to the side. Just a bit to the side often works very well. Don't believe it? Try putting something in the center of the quilt that you do not want to be dominant, and then attempt to make it less important. That is tricky! It can be done, but it is just better to avoid centering an item unless you are intent on emphatically featuring that element. Medallion quilts are

Scrutinizing a
Design

First-rate designs maintain their effectiveness in any direction. They can be turned or flipped and remain useable. Simply stated, a good design is a good design any way you look at it.

Can't figure out what's wrong with a design? Take a digital picture and turn it upside down. It is one way to study the design and find weaknesses.

Another way to study your design is by standing with your back to it with a mirror in hand. Looking at the reflection can show strengths and weaknesses.

Design 1 (pages 16–19), quilts Fine Feathered Friends and Floral Reflections, illustrates the fact that a good design can be rotated in various directions, producing different, effective quilts.

obvious examples of symmetry and centered focal points.

By grouping: Often, pulling together several items that are floating around will bring focus to the group as well as bring unity to the design (Figures 9–10).

Figure 9   Figure 10

In the section on balance (page 8), you saw that focus can be placed on a block by making it larger than the other elements. If you were to group several small elements, they could become a focal point and gain unity as well. Floating elements in figure 9 are grouped in figure 10 to improve the design.

By using dominant shapes: Circles and triangles are far more dominant and interesting than are squares and rectangles. Even smaller, more interesting shapes claim more attention than larger squares and rectangles.

By design line: Arrange elements so that an implied line leads the viewer's eye through the quilt to and from the focal point. This can be achieved by color as well as by block placement.

By a dominant color or dominant color value: Often, we quilters hear that color gets the credit but value does all the work. In fact, both play a part.

Contemplate Color
Success Factor:
Contrast in colors and values produces dynamic quilts.

What makes a color dominant? Why does one color seem to be more important than another?

First, you must realize that color is relative. That means that a color becomes dominant when it interacts with other colors beside it. It may be that one color is more pure than its neighbor. If a color is a shade (darkened) or a tint (lightened), it will be less important than its pure form.

Intensity is a big factor in producing dominant colors. Have you ever placed several colors alongside each other and noticed that some are so intense, so color saturated, that they leap off the table, leaving the others looking like wimps? Intensity does that, and balancing color intensity can make your quilt more appealing. Some of our contemporary quilts are composed completely of intense colors, and the results are invigorating and energizing.

A good way to balance intense colors is to add black. The use of black will provide a more level playing field for all the additional fabrics.

What happens if you add white? White is especially useful because it adds a sparkle to color combinations. It draws attention. That is why many quilters like combinations of one color plus white. Few people dislike blue and white quilts, or red and white, or black and white, or any other color plus white. The same reaction occurs with two colors plus white; a great example is the good old red, white, and blue combo.

To test this idea, pick two complementary colors from your fabric collection (purple and yellow, orange and blue, or red and green). Place the colors on a table alongside each other so that equal amounts of each are visible. Slide a piece of white beneath the two. You'll see that immediately, the white adds a zing.

Want a little less zing? Do the same with a light cream fabric and see what happens. It won't sparkle as much, but it will still offer a pleasant contrast.

The lesson learned is that the addition of neutrals can increase the dynamics of a quilt.

Additionally, be conscious of the size and amounts of white or cream that you use. Large sections of white can take over the quilt, which you would only want if you were planning to fill them with gorgeous quilting designs.

Color temperature is another factor that affects quilt dynamics. Warmer colors—the bright sunny oranges, reds, and yellows—will have the appearance of coming forward. Cooler colors—the blues and greens—are recessive and appear to move backward.

Sometimes a good way to add variety is to toss in a bright warm color amidst a sea of cooler colors. It will liven up things and add needed contrast. When varying color temperature, be aware that the amount of any color affects your results. Place a large amount of a warm orange on your quilt and it will become dominant. Make that color a dominant shape, such as round, and it can take command of the entire piece.

Guess what happens next. You have added the element of shape to color. Circles and quirky shapes grab the spotlight when used alongside squares, rectangles, and triangles. Change the size of these shapes and still something else may happen. I hope you are beginning to get the point, which is that you have a number of ways to add interest, variety, and focus to your quilt. Make something bigger or brighter, and it creates dominance. Balance it with something similar, either in shape, size, or color, and you're on a roll.

Play with Color and Value.

Try creating the following combinations using colors that you do not regularly use in your quilts. Do you have any emotional reactions to the combinations? Have you found some new favorites? I fully believe that you have to like the colors with which you are quilting. Otherwise, you will never like the quilt and you will regret the loss of time spent on it.

- *Select one color. Pull out every value of that color you have in your fabric resource center. Sort the fabric into piles of three values. Do you have*

Color
Vocabulary

Hue is another word for color.

Pure color indicates that no additional colors are present.

Complementary colors sit opposite each other on the color wheel.

Intensity is the degree of concentrated color. High intensity colors are saturated with pure color.

Shade is a color with added black.

Tint is a color with added white.

Tone is a color with added gray.

Temperature is a visual reaction to color. Yellow and red are warm; blue and green are cool. The temperature of a color is also relative. For instance, there can be cool reds and warm reds.

Value is lightness or darkness of a hue and is relative to its adjacent values.

light, medium, and dark values? If not, you may have to go shopping. (Oh dear!) This will show you if you generally lean toward purchasing fabrics of one value, which is often true of many quilters.

- Pick one color. Pull out its complement (for example, yellow and purple). Add white. Does this combination "sing?" Add two values of each of the colors. Has the chorus improved?

- Use either of these combinations and add a third color and two values of the added color.

Color
Exercise

Gene Ives, an experienced graphic artist and award-winning quilter, shares this exercise from a class on color.

Begin with a gray lake. Surround the lake with a seasonal color—for instance, wintry grays. Notice the effect on the color of the lake. Keeping the lake color constant, surround it with spring pastels, then the deep greens of summer, and finally the oranges of autumn.

As you switch the seasons, observe how your eye interprets the color of the lake and the changes that occur with each season. If you did not know otherwise, you would think that the color of the lake was changing, and it is all because our perception of color relies on the accompanying colors.

Understand Unity
Success Factor:
Unity gives viewers a comfortable feeling.

Unity, the feeling of "oneness," is achieved by effectively using balance, contrast, and focus. There is no magic formula, but the more you play with quilt design, the more unified your quilts will become. Graph paper, cut-out shapes, color samples, and computer quilt software could become your best friends as you try out your ideas.

A good way to "practice" unity is to study the pictures of quilts to which you have been drawn. You probably have a collection of magazine pictures, favorite books, and photographs from quilt shows. Lay them out and determine why you are drawn to them. It could be any number of reasons, probably more emotional than logical. Next, really look at them and seriously analyze what gives them unity.

One factor you may begin to notice is repetition. Designs are strengthened by repeating things—colors, lines, blocks, shapes, and sizes. Repetition of any element adds unity and harmony to a quilt. If you find yourself wondering what to do with a questionable area in a quilt design, repeat an element that you have already used. It is two for the price of one—you use repetition and gain unity.

Opposition strengthens a quilt as well. With the addition of opposing shapes, lines, or colors, a quilt gains more interest and can suddenly become very dynamic. A good example of opposition is to place varying color temperatures within blocks. Another way to add opposition is to use curved quilting designs in blocks or areas that feature straight lines; or use straight or diagonal line grids within circular areas.

As your quilt design progresses, consider all the factors discussed—balance, focus, color, and unity. Then, remember grandmother's adage that variety is the spice of life. Did she add that it is also the cinnamon and sugar on your quilts?

Some Assembly Required • Margie Engel

Success Factor:
Use what excites you—
your quilt is your quilt.

Anticipation meets action! The moment has come to begin your quilt. Start with a mental image of where you wish to go. Not an absolute, set-in-concrete pattern, mind you, but a general idea of what it is you wish to accomplish. Do you want to feature a fabric, a theme, a photograph, a feeling, or something else? It does not matter what you choose, but your project is going to be better if you pick one and then roll with it.

Follow your instincts. Trust them. Love them. Let them emerge. Give yourself credit, and don't worry if your friend does not get the point. All that matters is that you get it. You would be fortunate and wise to find some people who are designing their own quilts and look to them for reactions—not answers, but genuine observations.

Perhaps it is now time to pull out that delicious fabric that you've wanted to feature in a quilt. Pull out every additional fabric you have that you think will support the first fabric. Do this intuitively, as opposed to trying to use a particular color wheel scheme. Select a basic design from this book that appeals to you.

Start placing the colors alongside each other in the ways they will be used in the quilt. Face the fact that some will probably have to be eliminated. Decide if you would rather work with fewer fabrics so that you can repeat them throughout the quilt for the sake of unity. Do not be shocked if, down the quilt road, the original delicious fabric gets put aside. This happens sometimes. If so, you can begin another quilt with it; or you can work on two quilts simultaneously. Some folks enjoy dual processing.

Just for the sake of having a starting point, I am including a few of my favorite basic designs. You will note similarities in them. That is good. Then you will be able to change them to suit yourself and your ideas. Needless to say, they all utilize absolutely marvelous fabrics along with some duller ones that serve as supporting players. This is the moment to go into your fabric closet for those special fabrics that you had to buy simply because you had to have them! You liked them so well that you knew you would find a purpose for them someday. News flash: Someday is now!

In the designs, there are filler blocks. They are like the supporting roles in a drama. It takes more than one actor to create a play, and it takes additional blocks with secondary roles to produce a finished mixed techniques quilt. Some of my favorites are included. However, do not limit yourself to my choices—get your own favorites and insert them. (See the chapter on blocks, pages 50–61.)

Facilitate Your Quilt Planning
Design Wall

In addition to ideas and fabrics, you will need tools. You probably have most of them, but do you have a design wall? Once a nice thing to have, it is now a necessity! Viewing your quilt vertically makes a big difference in its outcome. Standing over it while it's arranged on the floor is not the best option, and moving the blocks around on the floor can be a hassle as well as physically challenging.

LEFT: FINE FEATHERED FRIENDS, detail. Full quilt on page 16.

The thousand-word picture: This is why you want and need a design wall!

The easiest, most immediate way to gain a design wall is to tape a piece of solid, neutral colored flannel or a flannel-backed tablecloth to a wall. The tape must be wide, at least 3" and to keep your wall unscathed, it should be painter's tape.

If you're serious about quilting and you have an available wall, it is ideal to have a permanent design wall. An easy way to get this is to purchase lightweight insulation material in 5' x 8' sheets. Cover them with flannel and mount them directly on the wall. I mount my design boards with T pins, hammered in at a slight downward angle, and

they have never fallen or slipped. Start at the top corner and space the pins about 10" apart; place about three across the center; then space more pins across the bottom. The material comes down easily in case you decide to move them, and the holes left in the wall are barely visible. With this wall, you are free to change block placement at the blink of an eye.

Digital Camera

Almost as necessary as a design wall is a digital camera—a very handy piece of equipment that promotes good decision-making. Keep one nearby.

It helps to be able to look at various arrangements in the camera because sometimes you cannot return to the former "better" arrangement unless you have a handy guide. Cameras offer great assistance when examining designs. They allow you to turn the photo sideways or upside down—the best views for evaluating a design. A good design can be turned in several directions and remain effective. This gives you multiple options, as shown in Design 1. Having several options is sometimes befuddling, but definitely beneficial.

Design Software

Computer quilt programs that truly aid the design process are readily available. Years ago, as a total computer novice, I purchased the first Electric Quilt® program (see Resources, page 94). Fortunately, it came with a well-written manual that provided an easy way to learn the program. I always purchase updates, which are relatively inexpensive considering their capabilities. Each update always brings additional help and excitement. Now it is a very sophisticated piece of software and absolutely necessary for my quilt designing.

If you are "into" computers, this is well worth the learning time. You may find yourself relaxing over the quilt program instead of playing computer solitaire.

Move from the Design Wall to Your Sewing Machine

Eventually, the moment arrives when you are ready to sew your quilt. Your design may be straightforward, allowing you to sew the blocks in horizontal rows that are then pressed and sewn together. Some of the designs in this book give opportunity for more strategic methods. Whatever the arrangement, use an organized system to keep the blocks in the correct orientation. Remove portions of the quilt from the wall, place them on the sewing table, recheck the arrangement, and sew. Some people prefer to number their blocks using masking tape to indicate the top left corner.

Add borders as the instructions or your inclinations require.

The great day finally comes when you have completed your quilt top. If you quilt your own quilts, then no doubt you have been thinking about this next step. I am an advocate of using both free-motion and machine-guided quilting, which I do on a domestic machine. If your quilts are to be put on a longarm quilt frame, you will note that in each design the fabric needs list batting and backing that are 8" larger than the quilt top. Be sure to check with your longarm quilter on the number of extra inches of batting and backing she recommends.

Should I mention that hand quilting is still treasured?

Use your favorite technique for adding the binding. Remember that you have additional choices. Some quilt artists are using facings to finish their small quilts. Many quilters are adding piping or accent flanges as well as binding. Though it is not alongside the binding, Design 5, JACOBEAN HOLIDAY (page 32) uses an accent flange around its center appliqué block.

Design 1:
Combine Appliqué and Strip-Set Blocks

The idea—feature tropical bird appliqués in a jungle atmosphere.

FINE FEATHERED FRIENDS, 46½" x 38", made by the author

Fabric Needs

Focus Fabric: 1 yard

Appliqué Backgrounds: ½ yard

Appliqués: 12" pieces for birds and various scraps for details

6" Strip-Set Block X Filler Blocks: ¼ yard each of 4 fabrics

Accent Bottom Border: ¼ yard

Borders: ⅜ yard if top and bottom borders are pieced; 1⅜ yards if borders are cut along the length of the fabric

Binding: ⅜ yard

Backing: 2¾ yards (piece crosswise)

Batting: 54" x 46"

Tropical birds are born with the appearance of having individual personalities. The next best thing to having a parrot is having one that does not squawk—hence, the appliqué. My quest for a focus fabric imparting a jungle feeling was rewarded with a fabric with a variety of gorgeous greens and a bonus of several tropical birds sitting among the greenery. All I needed to do was draw three large birds for appliqué (see the appliqué patterns, pages 71–74). For supporting blocks, I used Strip-Set Block X (pages 52–54).

Cutting Instructions

The appliqué background and focus fabrics are also used in the strip blocks, so the larger pieces are cut first.

If your focus fabric is directional, begin by cutting the left side piece vertically (6½" x 18½"), then the top right horizontal piece (18½" x 6½"), then the 6½" square (used on the bottom row of the quilt). Use the remainder for cutting strips for blocks.

Cut the appliqué background fabric beginning with a 13" wide piece cut selvage to selvage. From this, cut three 13" squares.

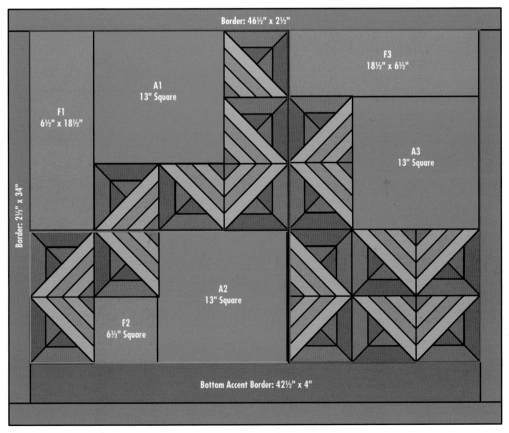

Cutting *measurements and assembly diagram*

Stitching the Appliqués

These appliqués are highlighted with Prismacolor® Premier Colored Pencils. This raw-edged method relies on applying fusible interfacing to the back of the appliqué before it is embellished and added to the background (see the section on using appliqué, pages 68–70).

The appliqués are machine sewn to the background fabric, usually with a blanket stitch using matching and variegated threads and a sharp needle.

After completing the appliqués, size these blocks to squares 12½" x 12½". Use the remaining fabric for cutting strips for blocks.

Making the Blocks

Consult the instructions for the 6" finished Block X (pages 52–54) and make 16.

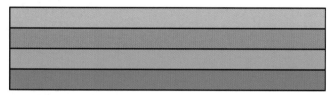

Strip-Set 1 — Make 2

Strip-Set 2 — Make 4

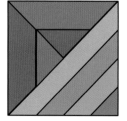

Block X — Make 16

Sew all your blocks, including the appliqués, and lay them out on your design wall. If you prefer, the focus fabric sections can be filled with supporting blocks.

Assembling the Quilt

Consult the quilt diagram and note the 3 sections boxed by the colored lines. The colored lines are not part of the quilt; they serve to visually designate the 3 assembly units.

Sew the upper left-hand portion, outlined in red, by joining 2 filler blocks and sewing them to the bottom of appliqué block A1. Join the 3 blocks to the right of A1 to each other and sew them to the A1 section. Complete the unit by attaching focus fabric F1 as shown in the diagram.

The lower section, outlined in green, is assembled in similar manner and then sewn to the top section.

Complete the right-hand section (outlined in blue), then sew to the left-hand portion of the quilt.

For the accent border on the bottom, measure your quilt horizontally through the middle. Cut the fabric to equal that measurement. Pin the accent border to the quilt in the middle and ends of the quilt and stitch them together.

For the side borders, measure your quilt vertically through the middle. Cut the fabric to equal that measurement and continue as you did for the accent border. Repeat this process for the top and bottom borders.

Stand back, admire your work, and proceed with adding batting and backing. Look closely and you will notice machine-guided quilting among the strips and free-motion quilting around the birds. Use your favorite binding method.

Design 1 Variations

Remember the premise that a good design will be effective in any direction? Let's turn this design sideways. Ask yourself the "What if?" question and change this design to accommodate your tastes.

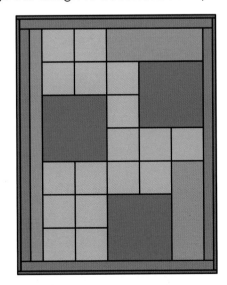

Design 1 turned sideways

Another quilt rotation, a few simple changes, and added sashes around the blocks produce a very appealing variation of Design 1.

Design 1 variation with sashes

Compare FLORAL REFLECTIONS with the figure above. You will see that instead of sashing each block, I sewed sashes to sections of combined blocks. The left-hand border just happened while I was playing with the leftovers from the strip-sets.

FLORAL REFLECTIONS, 34" x 42", made by the author;
Design 1 variation with Strip-Set Block Y fillers

Design 2: Blend a Pre-Printed Panel with Filler Blocks

The idea—fabric panels can be cut apart and used creatively in original designs.

SPLASH, *46" x 48", made by the author*

Fabric Needs

1 pre-printed fabric panel

Strip-set blocks: ¼ yard each of
5* coordinating fabrics

Top Border and strips: ¼ yard

Side Borders and strips: ½ yard

Binding: ⅜ yard

Backing: 3¼ yards

Batting: 54" x 56"

*Any number of fabrics can be used for the strip-set blocks; you may choose to use one strip each of numerous fabrics.

Many printed panels are produced as ready-made projects, but they can also provide additional fun for quilters who adapt them for use in larger quilts. Wanting a quilt reminiscent of the beach, I searched for a seascape. My find was a busy ocean scenario with many fish, whales, and coral. The best part of the panel was the top section with two dolphins leaping out of the water. Added fabrics featuring turtles and streaming dolphins maintained the ocean theme, so the only remaining needs were fabrics with different values for the strip-set blocks.

I used both the X and Y strip-set blocks. Additional fish from other fabrics are appliquéd onto the quilt.

You can duplicate this pattern with any panel that can be advantageously cut into sections. Add coordinating fabrics and move on to sheer bliss.

Cutting Instructions

Begin by scrutinizing your panel to determine what portions you would like to use and how they can be cut. In SPLASH, I began by selecting the 10½" squares C, E, and H (see lettered diagram below). Then I selected areas B, F, and J. Other sections of the panel were later used in piecing the side blocks and as appliqués near the bottom of the quilt. I cut the squares first, and then the other pieces. Square D was cut from a separate turtle fabric.

Cut your panel to match the dimensions given in the cutting diagram or adjust the measurements as needed. If your panel sections are smaller than the ones shown, add sashing strips and then trim them to size.

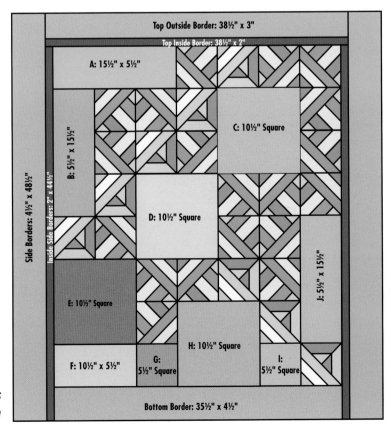

Cutting measurements and assembly diagram

Making the Blocks

Strip-Set 1 — Make 1

Strip-Set 2 — Make 2

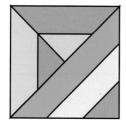

Block X — Make 8

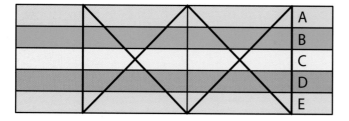

Strip-Set 3 — Make 2 — Cut as shown

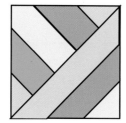

Block Y — Make 19

Lay out the panel pieces on your design wall. Determine which filler blocks you would like to use. Do not overlook the idea of using squares of coordinating fabrics.

Construct some samples of your filler blocks and audition them with your panel cuts. Rely on your instincts, decide what you like, then finish constructing your pieced blocks. Refrain from cutting long filler sections from your panel until you have read the next paragraph!

Assembling the Quilt

Make a quick diagram of your planned quilt if it varies from the design shown. Sew the quilt in units. Once you get started, it will become easier than it appears at the outset. If you see areas that will be easier to sew by dividing the longer strips, cut them, adding seam allowance. Remember, too, that any small area in the pre-print that you don't like may easily be disguised with an appliqué.

After the interior of your quilt is finished, audition border fabrics and decide how many you wish to use. Experiment with various possibilities. My favorite part of SPLASH was adding a third dolphin—an appliqué version of the dolphins in the fabric that I drew with colored pencils—and using scraps from the panel to assemble the outside borders.

Continue the fun—add batting and backing, quilt, and finish the binding to suit your fancy.

RIGHT: SPLASH, detail. Full quilt on page 20.

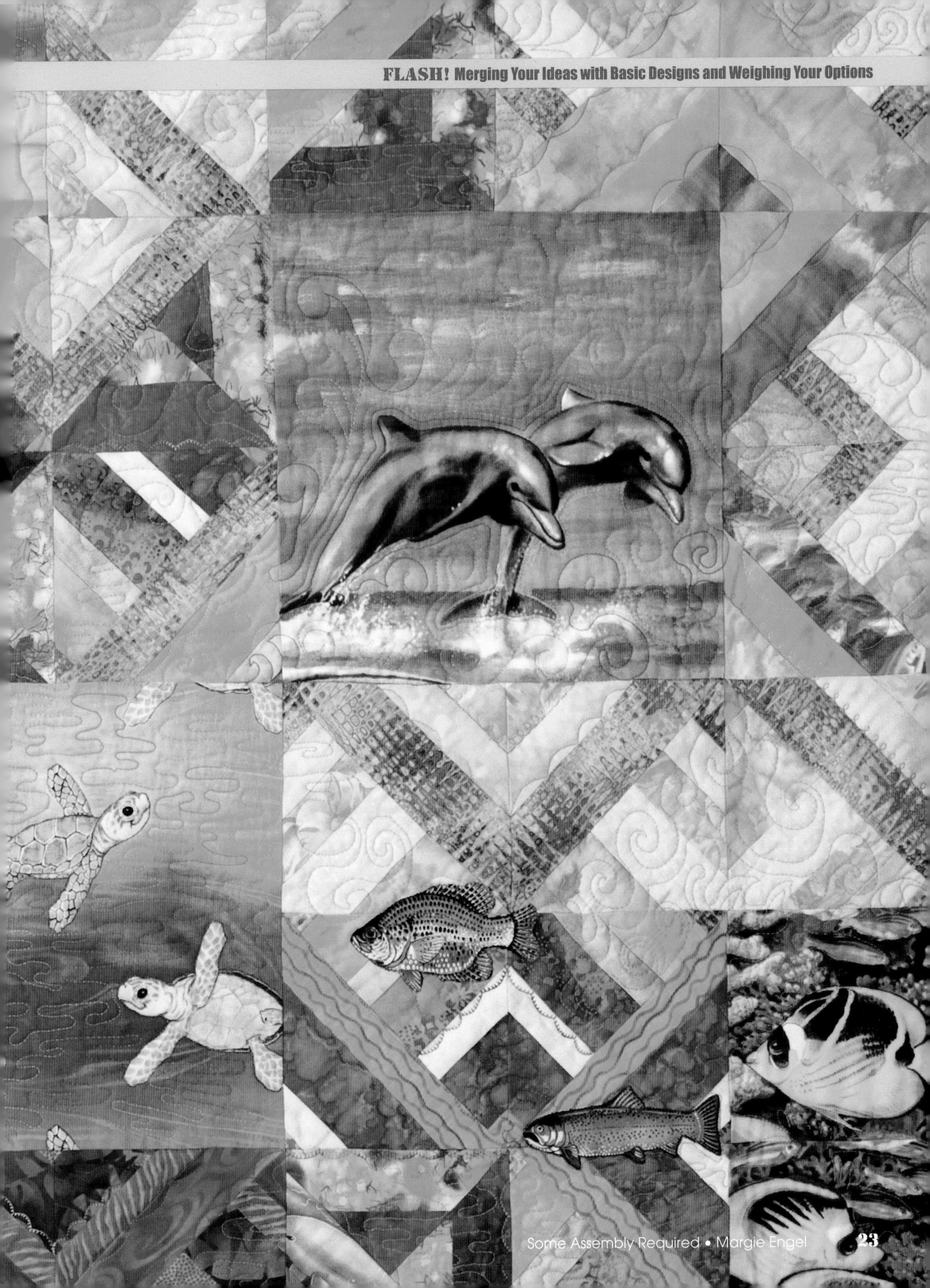

Design 3: Highlight Large-Scale Fabrics in Big Blocks

The idea—breathtaking fabric can set the mood for a dynamic quilt.

Eyes on the Serengeti, 55" x 67", made by the author

Fabric Needs

Large-scale print focus fabrics: ½ yard and ⅜ yard each of 2 prints (⅞ yard total); the amounts may vary based on the pattern repeat

Strip-Set Block Z strips: ¼ yard each of 5 fabrics

Center strips in Block Z and fill fabric beside 8" strip blocks: ⅜ yard

Sashes: ⅜ yard

Pieced blocks in side borders: ¾ yard each of 2 fabrics

Top & bottom borders and bottom center block: ½ yard

Binding: ½ yard

Backing: 4 yards

Batting: 63" x 75"

The large-scale African animal print leapt from the shelf into my arms! At that moment, I knew that the soulful zebras would have a prominent place in a quilt soon to be born. It did not take long to figure out the design, which called for strip-set blocks and machine-embroidered sections. The strips offered great opportunity to use machine-guided decorative stitches for quilting.

To repeat the triangle shape in the side blocks, I drew a quilting design that worked in the borders, as well as in the animal blocks, and welcomed beads. I looked forward to finishing the quilting, knowing that when the quilting was done, extensive beadwork could begin. Oh joy! My collection of African beads finally found a home.

Note the symmetrical design and the use of warm colors with the addition of blue. Even though blue is a cool color, relatively speaking this blue is warm.

Top Border: 55½" x 4"
6½" Square
12½" x 11½"
2" x 13½"
13½" x 16½"
2" x 13½"
12½" x 11½"
6½" Square
12½" x 2"
3¾" x 5½"
6" x 5½"
3¾" x 5½"
12½" x 2"
3¾" x 5½"
6" x 5½"
3¾" x 5½"
12½" x 2"
16½" x 2"
12½" x 2"
6½" x 1½"
3¼" x 8½"
2¾" x 8½"
6½" x 6½"
2¾" x 8½"
3¼" x 8½"
6½" x 1½"
2" x 60½"
8½" x 8½"
8½" x 8½"
16½" x 2"
4½" x 16½"
8½" x 8½"
2" x 15½"
13½" x 15½"
2" x 15½"
8½" x 8½"
4½" x 16½"
2" x 60½"
12½" x 11½"
12½" x 11½"
12½" x 2½"
6½" x 6½"
6½" x 6½"
16½" x 18½"
6½" x 6½"
6½" x 6½"
12½" x 2½"
12½" x 2½"
12½" x 2½"
12½" x 4½"
12½" x 4½"
Bottom Border: 55½" x 4"

Cutting measurements and assembly diagram. For an unlabeled piece, refer to its opposite position for the cutting size.

Making the Blocks

Four 8" Z Blocks are used in the center portion of the quilt and four 6" Z Blocks are used near the bottom. Refer to the Block Z instructions (pages 56–57).

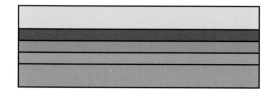

6" Block Z Strip-Set — Make 2

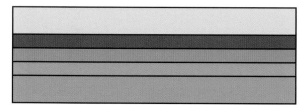

8" Block Z Strip-Set — Make 2

6" Block Z
Make 4

8" Block Z
Make 4

Assembling the Quilt

This design is sewn in 3 vertical units. The side borders are made with quarter-square triangles (see page 58).

Near the top of the quilt, small embroidered animal heads in the side units have blocks on either side that are assembled from remnants of the strip-sets. This idea is repeated on the sides of the elephant just under the zebra in the center section. That elephant is a purchased textile, but could easily be found in another fabric. The animal blocks to the left and right of the zebras came from a different fabric, so you will note a color variation.

This quilt encourages you to pull out all your theme fabrics and use them in various ways. If the background of a particular fabric does not work well with the focus fabric, cut out the part you like, apply an adhesive, and appliqué it, which is the story of the two elephants on the quilt's lower right side.

EYES ON THE SERENGETI, *detail, lower center block*

The tiger eyes are embroidered on felt and the zebra eyes are stitched on commercial zebra abric. Both embroideries are topstitched to the block fabric (see page 68). The faces are from a swatch of an authentic African textile, also topstitched to the block. Note the use of beads within the quilting design.

Embroidery source: Animal Instincts, produced by Oklahoma Embroidery Supply & Design (see Resources, page 94).

RIGHT: EYES ON THE SERENGETI, detail. Full quilt on page 24.

Design 4: Produce Excitement with Bold Colors and Serendipitous Arranging

The idea—combine black-and-white fabrics with bodacious colors.

SOME ASSEMBLY REQUIRED, 57" x 65", made by the author

Fabric Needs

Strip-Set 1: 3 yards total assorted fabrics

Strip-Set 2: 1¼ yards each of 2 fabrics

Inside Border: ¼ yard cut into 6 strips 1½" wide

Outside Border: ⅔ yard cut into 6 strips 3½" wide

Binding: ½ yard

Backing: 4 yards

Batting: 65" x 73"

This quilt design and its name came into existence simultaneously too many years ago with the promise that someday I would get around to sewing it. After several Christmas Eves passed with repeated giggles over instructions labeled "Some Assembly Required," I finally fulfilled my promise and had way too much fun making this quilt. It should be approached with reckless abandon and a willingness to let it take you where it wants to go!

If you demand matched points everywhere, you will only get that by carefully cutting your block parts and by cutting the strips all the same width. If you understand that quilts like this are not akin to making Star blocks that need points, then you can relax and enjoy the pleasures of arranging these blocks on a design wall, knowing that some blocks will meet and match, and others, when rotated twice, may not. Remember to take a photograph of every change, as it is almost impossible to return to an original starting point without a picture.

If you prefer symmetrical arrangements, take a look at FLOWER POWER in the gallery (page 88) so you can weigh your options. You will observe that strip blocks placed symmetrically produce interesting visual patterns.

Assembly diagram

Making the Blocks

Follow the instructions for 8" (finished size) Block X (pages 52–54).

Strip-Set 1 — Make 7

Strip-Set 2 — Make 12

8" Block X — Make 39

To sew the strip-sets, I cut strips from a large variety of fabrics and hung them over the rods of a drying rack. I selected the strips as I sewed, picking colors that were good neighbors and played together well. With no criteria, I gleefully stitched, only mindful of maintaining quarter-inch seams. You can do the same.

I applied fabric sizing to the sets and let them air dry before cutting them into triangles. (I actually practice what I preach—using fabric sizing on your strip-sets prevents distortion, as discussed in the block directions, page 51.) There are 39 X Blocks and 3 odd blocks made with strip-set leftovers.

Three odd blocks make a good background for the appliquéd flowers.

Check the photograph and you will see that I maintained the black/white pattern for strip-set 2. I felt that using repetitive colors would give some unity to the piece and provide some resting places for the viewers' eyes. Busy quilts benefit when there is a quiet moment among the noise of numerous colors and lines.

Assembling the Quilt

The merriment continues with completed blocks. It is easy to find several arrangements when using a design wall. Selecting just one is the challenge. This is where the digital camera becomes invaluable. When you find an arrangement you like, take a picture. This leaves you free to experiment, knowing you can always refer to the photos to return to a former arrangement.

While playing at the design wall, it occurred to me that tab inserts would be an interesting addition and provide an opportunity for adding buttons. Little did I know this idea was just the beginning. Once the button box was open, the quilt borders became an irresistible place for all the buttons I'd saved. If you like the inserted tabs, see Envelope Flaps and Tab Inserts (pages 59–60). Use fabric squares cut 2½" x 2½" for the smaller flaps and 3½" x 3½" for the larger ones.

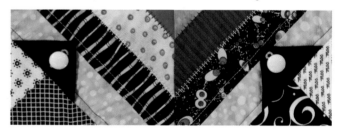

The embroidered appliqués were made with 2 methods—one using felt and the other using tulle in a hoop. (See pages 68–70, Using Appliqué.)

Embroidery Source for black-and-white flowers: Funky Flowers by Margit Grimm, produced by Husqvarna Viking (see Resources, page 94).

After the quilt top is finished, add embellishments such as rickrack. Add batting and backing, quilt the top, and attach the buttons. The final step is binding the quilt.

SOME ASSEMBLY REQUIRED, machine embroidery appliqué detail. Full quilt on page 28.

Design 5: Focus on Extraordinary Elements

The idea—machine embroidery is a "Wow!" companion for appliqués.

Jacobean Holiday, 47" x 42", made by the author

Design option: Consider replacing the embroidered squares with your favorite pieced blocks, squares of beautiful fabrics, or other types of fiber art.

Is it not amazing that our domestic sewing machines have the capability to produce gorgeous embroi-

dery? Once these machines became available to the home sewer, it was only a matter of time before this technique was incorporated into our quilts.

Having seen many Jacobean types of embroidery that used wool, I decided to try felt as the back-

Fabric Needs

Embroidery Backgrounds: ¾ yard felt (includes extra for hooping)

Sashes for embroidered squares: ⅜ yard

Sashes and Borders (checked fabric in photo): ⅔ yard

Appliqué Backgrounds: ⅔ yard

Appliqués: ½ yard total of various fabrics for flowers, leaves, and stems

Stabilizer: ⅔ yard

Binding: ⅜ yard

Backing: 3 yards

Batting: 55" x 50"

ground for the embroidered motifs. It worked very well, offering excellent stability for the dense stitching as well as allowing the thread to stand out. In addition, the felt provided a firm base for beading.

If you have decided that you like symmetrical designs, not only does this fit the description, but it is also an easy quilt to assemble. The primary decision is determining the size of the embroidered motifs and the subsequent required size of the background squares. If your designs require larger squares, then you may have to reduce the number of squares if you are still going to use the central appliqué.

Assembling the Quilt

Complete the embroideries and the appliqués and cut the blocks to the appropriate sizes. Sew the quilt in 3 sections. Consult the cutting diagram and cut the fabrics for the center portion of the quilt, in this instance the fabrics surrounding the 3 top embroideries and the 2 appliqué blocks. Assemble the center unit. Measure the length of that section vertically to determine the length of the embroidery panels on either side.

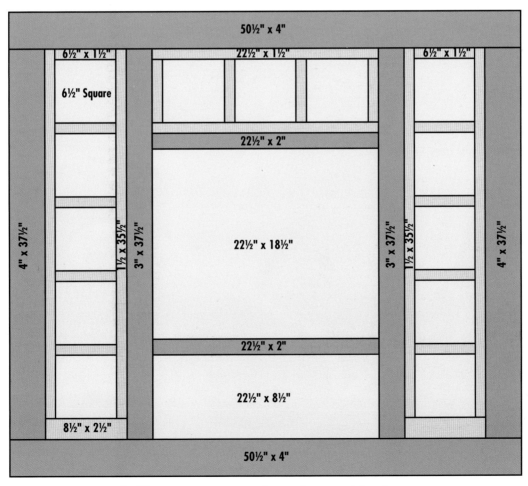

Cutting *measurements and assembly diagram*

A half-inch wide flange is inserted around the center appliqué block. If you opt for this addition, cut a strip of fabric twice the desired width plus ½" for the seam allowance (1½" in this instance). Cut 4 lengths equal to the side of the raw-edged block. Fold the strips in half lengthwise, wrong sides together. Align the raw edges of the strips with the raw edges of the block fabrics and baste. Apply the border fabric. The accent strip lies flat, facing into the block and doing its job, which is to highlight the area it surrounds.

Each side panel has the same measurements. Study the diagram and note that the bottom sash on the embroidery panels is larger than the top sash. Also, the top sash of each embroidery block is sewn to the embroidered square before the side sashes are attached. The bottom sash is sewn across the entire panel bottom (8½" wide, unfinished) after the side sashes are attached. This is so you can change the height of the bottom sash to fit the measurement of your center panel. Complete the embroidered panel except for the bottom sash; measure it vertically. Compare its height to your central unit and make any necessary adjustments.

Sew all 3 sections together, attach the borders, and you are on your way to quilting your masterpiece! Add backing and batting and use your favorite binding technique.

Embroidery Source: Crewel Embroidery by Iris Lee, produced by Oklahoma Embroidery Supply & Design (see Resources, page 94).

JACOBEAN HOLIDAY, details. Full quilt on page 32.

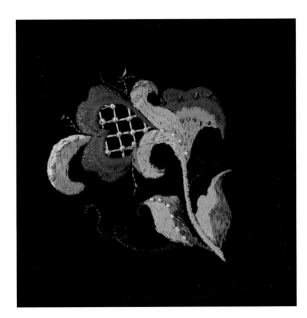

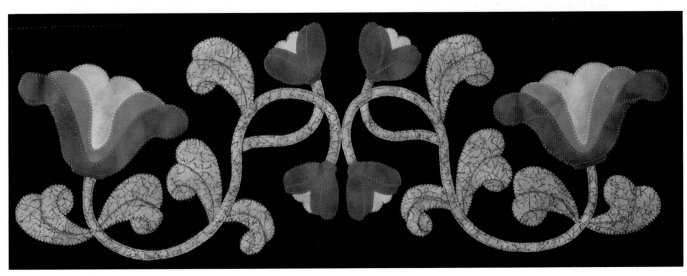

Design 6: Use Special Effects for a Unique Quilt

The idea—Oh, yes! Trapunto adds elegance and interesting texture to quilts.

THIS NEW DAY, 27" x 39", made by the author

Fabric Needs

Trapunto: ¼ yard

Light color for blocks: ¾ yard

Filler rectangles: ⅜ yard

Drunkard's Path small sections: 13 – 4½" x 4½" squares of various fabrics

Binding: ⅜ yard

Backing: 1⅓ yards

Batting: 31" x 43"

THIS NEW DAY grew from the desire to focus on a long trapunto design. Initially, I planned a white trapunto panel because I love the elegance of white stitching on white fabric. However, the white was overbearing because the panel was so large, even when I stippled with a pale green thread around the trapunto. There lies the proof that large focal pieces can be overwhelming when done in white or yellow. I switched to a pale blue fabric, since blue is a recessive color, and found the results more suitable.

The stitching done around a trapunto design has a purpose, which is to promote the trapunto and push it forward. There are various ways to achieve this. One method is to quilt a grid pattern, but that requires a great number of starts and stops—not too smart with this involved design. Echoing the design can work, but, again, there's an easier way. Good old stippling, the easy free-motion quilting, works every time when the desired effect is to promote a design. But wait! Stippling creates another dilemma.

Stippling around trapunto results in a great deal of stitch density. This can create a problem when the trapunto is positioned in the interior of a quilt. Knowing this, I decided that I would add a very thin layer of batting to the trapunto panel and stipple it before sewing the quilt top together. This method left me room for later decisions about quilting that would not be dictated by the trapunto panel's density.

True, quilting would still be needed in the panel, but that could be achieved by duplicating some stitching with monofilament. I am never sure that going against what I know to be true will work, but my adventurous spirit always encourages my trying things out. This time it worked, but extra effort was required to keep the fabrics smooth during quilting. Next time, I'll try the traditional route—create the trapunto, sew the block into the quilt, then quilt the entire piece. After all, isn't that the safest way?

Your stand on this issue is the next story to be told.

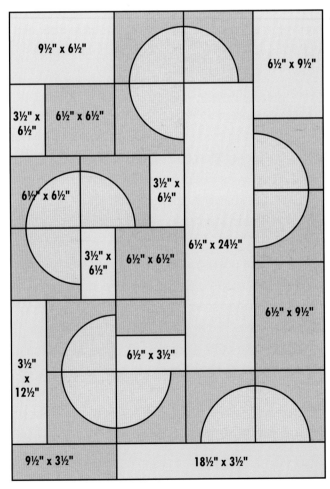

Cutting *measurements and assembly diagram*

Cutting Instructions

Drunkard's Path blocks don't get nearly the credit they deserve. Since they are built around a quarter circle, they offer intriguing opportunities to suggest circles without having to make a complete circle. These blocks and a few daisies offered pleasant surroundings for the trapunto.

There are 13 Drunkard's Path blocks among the plain blocks. Block directions are on pages 58–59 and the daisies and trapunto design are in the appliqué pattern section (page 78). To make the quilt, you need only consult the diagram, as it is very quick and easy once the trapunto is completed.

Trapunto Techniques

Trapunto adds elegance and texture to quilts. It is a puffy quilting design produced by padding the quilting design with batting. Achieving effective trapunto requires good lighting, patience, and two different types of scissors. Patience is needed to snip away excess filling because big scissor chops promote disastrous results. Blunt-ended scissors are good for the initial cutting away as they won't put holes in your fabric. Sharper scissors are needed to cut away filling that is close to the design lines. Duckbill scissors work very well, but keep the duckbill parallel to the fabric with the pointed scissor blade on the design side.

Be aware that batting is used for different functions in this quilt. The trapunto filling is polyester batting, the thicker the better. Use more than one layer for added thickness. You can use several layers of cotton batting if you insist, but it is not as puffy, and the cotton requires longer air-drying time.

The second batting is used for the entire quilt. Select your favorite fiber. I prefer cotton.

Use a water-soluble marker to draw the design onto your fabric. This marker becomes permanent when exposed to heat, so press the fabric before drawing on it and after rinsing out the marker. Do not use any detergents or soaps when rinsing out the marker. Just thoroughly soak the marked fabric, using a large amount of cold water.

For a long time, I stitched trapunto as I was taught, using water-soluble thread for the perimeter of the design before cutting away the unwanted filling, then doing a second stitching that was permanent. Because I like large, detailed trapunto, stitching twice became tedious. I did what I tell my students to do—ask the "What if..." question. What if I stitch only once with permanent thread, then cut out away the excess filling? The results were favorable. So, stitch once if you choose, but read on before you do.

Another tactic I learned is to use a slightly darker color thread in the bobbin. It is much easier to see the stitches amid the puffy filling and avoid snipping them when cutting around the design. When I decided to only stitch once, I learned the risks. With second stitching planned, you can concentrate on snipping away filling and not think twice if you accidentally snip a stitch because it is basting thread that is going to be replaced. If you stitch only once, the snipped stitch has to be repaired by taking a section out, restitching, and pulling the threads to the back to be knotted. Only you can decide how you wish to approach this wonderful technique.

Gosh, is it worth all this? Yes, if you love the effects of trapunto, and I do. Obviously, you could take the same design, turn it into a fusible appliqué and achieve great results. This is your quilt and you get to select your own options.

The end is in sight. Add batting and backing; quilt your favorite designs or use the ginkgo pattern on page 78. Bind, using your favorite method.

RIGHT: THIS NEW DAY, detail. Full quilt on page 36.

Design 7: Display Favorite Photographs

The idea—just a whim; photograph stuffed animals for a dustless collection.

FUR & FLUFF, 47" x 57", made by the author

In this exciting world of electronics, digital cameras have claimed a significant place in quilting. Many quilters are delighted to add photography to quilts, especially since pretreated fabric sheets for printing directly from computers are available (see Resources, page 94). These have been so well-developed that even a novice can achieve wonderful results as long as she reads and follows the directions that accompany the fabric.

Some quilters prefer to cut their own fabric and soak it in a setting solution. This is less expensive than the commercially treated fabric but requires more prep time and effort. The forerunner to these methods is the transfer fabric that allows you to print the photograph on transfer paper and iron it to fabric.

The primary requirement is a good digital photograph. Recognize that almost every photograph is improved by cropping, which means removing unnecessary areas around the subject. Too often, peripheral elements distract from what could be a very effective photo. Close cropping allows the subject to be larger in the printout. It also helps when sizing the photograph to suit your layout. Sharpen the image if needed and print it first on paper. If you are happy with the results, print it on the fabric.

The second requirement is to decide what size to print the photographs. I chose 8" x 10" photos, some printed in landscape mode (horizontal), others in portrait mode (vertical). Both modes need an added strip sewn on one side to produce 10" blocks for the quilt.

Fabric selection for photograph quilts requires judicious value choices. Your fabrics should complement the photographs and keep them in the forefront. It is possible that high-intensity fabrics will detract from the photos, so you might prefer to select calmer colors.

In developing the design for Fur & Fluff, I wanted blocks as playful as the stuffed bears; because bears are furry, I wanted texture. What better way to achieve both ideas than to use a textured pinwheel? My method is to sew the easy Envelope block (pages 59–60) and tuck the flap into the seam. Group 4 blocks together, each rotated 90 degrees from its neighbor, and you have a playful pinwheel! Hmmm…

Fabric Needs

7 pretreated photo fabric sheets, 8½" x 11"
Orange: ½ yard
Light Brown: ½ yard
Cream: 1 yard
Dark Brown print: ¾ yard
Pale Orange: ½ yard
Inner Border: ¼ yard
Outer Border: ½ yard
Binding: ½ yard
Backing: 3⅞ yards
Batting: 55" x 65"

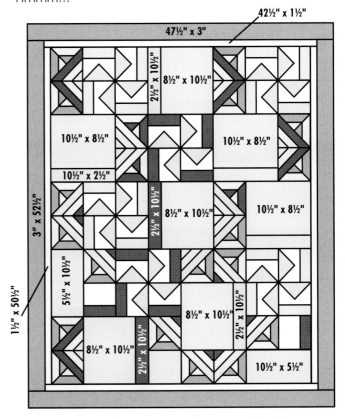

***Cutting** measurements and assembly diagram*

What if I were to add my favorite strip-set blocks? With no hesitation, I was off and running to the design wall.

To create your own photograph quilt, begin by positioning the photographs on your design wall. Try out various fabrics to see what brings out the best in the photos. Then sew sample blocks and try those out in the same manner.

FUR & FLUFF features seven 8" x 10" photographs on fabric, which are accompanied by 5" x 5" Envelope blocks with flaps (24), 5" x 5" Envelope blocks without flaps (2), X Blocks (21), and fabric fillers (2 measuring 5" x 10" and one 5" x 5" square).

Making the Blocks

Complete the Envelope blocks and baste the raw edges of the flaps to the raw edges of the blocks. Combine 24 of these blocks into four-patch units, rotating each block 90 degrees from its neighbor to produce the pinwheel effect shown in the diagram. (Consult the block instructions, pages 59–60.)

Make the 2 "flapless" Envelope blocks, the X blocks, and the fillers.

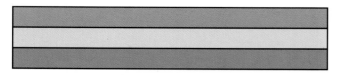

Strip-Set 1 — Make 2

Strip-Set 2 — Make 3

Block X — Make 21

Assembling the Quilt

Position all of the elements, and then consult the diagram to see how they were sewn. The assembly begins with sewing 3 horizontal rows and then changes to sewing sections at the bottom of the quilt.

Two borders finish the quilt and it is ready for batting, backing, quilting, and binding.

RIGHT: FUR & FLUFF, detail. Full quilt on page 40.

Design 8: Recycle Jeans Pockets

The idea—start a trend; cut up old jeans and rescue the pockets for your quilts.

POCKETS, PLAIDS, AND PINWHEELS, 38" x 47", made by the author

Fabric Needs

All the blocks: 2 yards total of various fabrics
      8 jeans pockets

Small scraps: for appliqués

Inner Borders: ⅜ yard

Outer Border: ½ yard

Binding: ⅜ yard

Backing: 3¼ yards

Batting: 46" x 55"

Recycling jeans pockets is a longtime favorite pastime of mine, so I keep them readily available. If you do not have a built-in supply, second-hand retail shops always have a preponderance of jeans that are very inexpensive. Team the pockets with scrap fabrics for a winning quilt. My leftovers produced a surprising number of plaids and stripes, fabrics that always seem to blend well with denim.

Selecting the plaids was a no-brainer. However, cutting them so that the lines were straight was another challenge since plaids, even woven ones, are not always on grain. Heed this as a warning if you, too, select plaids and stripes. On the other hand, since the pockets and pinwheels are tilted, why should a few slanted plaids bother us?

Since pockets serve to hold things, I thought it would be great fun to have critters crawling out of them. In keeping with the pocket idea, and just because I like to sew dimensional inserts into quilts, I sewed Tab Inserts into some of the filler fabric rectangles. The same element is in Design 4 (page 28) and is detailed in the blocks chapter (page 60).

Whimsical designs welcome creative borders. You have the option of adding basic borders to this design or to adopt the checkerboard idea. I love checkerboards and add them whenever they fit with the quilt. They take a little additional time, but are no big deal when a masterpiece is underway. Besides, this book is supposed to give you ideas—

some you will like, others you will disregard. Same story—your quilt is your quilt!

Design and Cutting Measurements

Pocket Backgrounds: 8 squares 9½" x 9½"

9 rectangles 9½" x 5"

1 square 5" x 5"

Tabs on square and rectangle blocks: 6 squares 3" x 3"

Dancing Pinwheel blocks:

6 squares 4" x 4" of one fabric

6 squares 4" x 4" of contrasting fabric

4 strips 3½" wide cut selvage to selvage for pinwheel borders, trimmed to size after sewing

Borders are cut selvage to selvage and include strips for the checkerboards.

Inner border:

6 strips 1½" wide

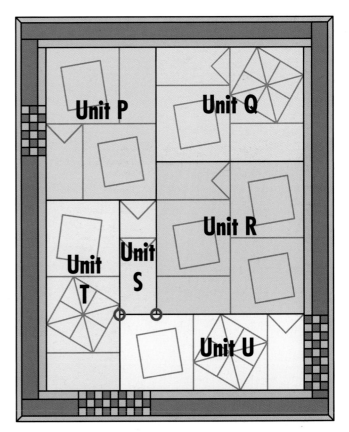

Assembly diagram; circles indicate partial seams

Outer border:
2 strips 1½" wide
4 strips 2½" wide

Here we go. This is one time to be sure to read all the directions first!

The whimsical appearance of this quilt emerges for two reasons—the tilt of the pockets and pinwheels and the offset blocks (as opposed to all the blocks arranged in rows). If design is everything, then a method for sewing this has to be figured out.

Partial Seams

The Useful Replacement for Set-in Seams

A partial seam is sewn in 2 steps. The first step is to sew part of the seam, stopping to allow enough movement for the other end of the seam. Other seams in adjacent areas are completed, and then the completion of the partial seam finishes joining blocks or portions of blocks.

Partial seam in progress

The results were worth it to me, but before you decide to use this block arrangement, read the section on assembling the quilt (page 47). Set-in blocks are avoided by using partial seaming. If this technique is new to you, then perhaps this is a good time to learn it. The results will give you new design freedom in the future because you won't need to twiddle with inset seams. (A "Hooray!" from you would be appropriate now.)

But wait—this is your quilt. If you prefer easier methods, draw your own arrangement (this is a design book isn't it?) or skip to the Design 8 Variations (page 48), and you can still enjoy all the other parts of this quilt!

Making the Blocks

Prepare pockets by removing them from the jeans. This involves patiently tearing out all the stitches. Many pockets have decorative stitching on them, which can be left intact, enhanced, or removed. I like to add decorative stitches to the pockets in bright-colored threads.

Do not try to remove any brads on the pocket corners, but know that they will require some hand stitching at the tops to secure them to the quilt. You might opt to select only pockets without brads. Set the pockets aside. These will be attached later.

Cut all the fabrics and arrange them as you like. Take a photo of your arrangement for later reference.

If you are adding Tab Inserts to your quilt, refer to page 60 and use 3" x 3" squares. Baste the tabs onto the filler rectangles and sew in place.

Piece the Dancing Pinwheel blocks (see pages 60–61). This quilt uses 6½" raw-edge pinwheels within the 9½" block (9" finished).

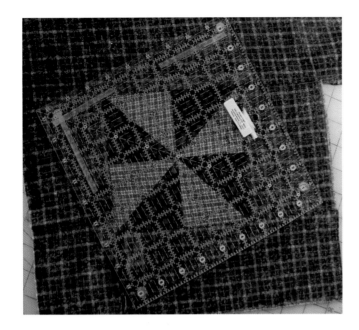

If you are adding appliqués, sew the quilt blocks together in sections that provide the needed space for the critters. Refer to the photograph and the assembly diagram. Temporarily pin the pocket to the block so that you can see where to position the appliqué. Remove the pocket and stitch the appliqué.

Assembling the Quilt

Consult the assembly diagram and complete the sections as indicated by various colors.

Pin the pockets into position and stitch them down. Since you have removed the original stitching from the pockets, the stitching lines will be visible. Most jeans pockets have 2 rows of stitching. Decide how you want to stitch these. I usually sew on those visible lines. If you opted for pockets with brads in the corners, after doing the machine stitching, you will need to anchor those corners by hand.

Machine stitch the pocket for 1" along the top. Position an open-toe foot along the pocket edge and stitch toward the brad. The stitches keep the pocket functional while only slightly minimizing the pocket opening.

Sew each section in the order shown, using partial seams where circled. (Truthfully, the directions were harder to write than the actual sewing, so hang in here with me.)

1. Stitch unit Q to unit R.

2. Stitch blue unit S to gray unit T, stopping 2" from the bottom of the S unit.

3. Stitch S/T unit to above orange unit P.

4. Stitch S/P units to Q/R units.

5. Stitch the bottom portion of gray unit T to yellow unit U, beginning at the bottom and stitching about 6". This seam stops about 3" down from the top of the U unit.

6. Stitch Unit U to R, beginning at the right sides of the quilt and sewing to the end of the Dancing Pinwheel block in U.

7. Stitch the left sides of S to U for 3".

8. Complete the S/T seam.

9. Complete the R/U seam.

10. Shout "Hooray!" and pat yourself on the back.

Decide what kind of borders you prefer. Assuming you survived learning to partially seam the sections, how difficult can a pieced border be? The directions for the checkerboards are on pages 57–58.

Check out the borders in the photograph that show the results of sewing both borders together before attaching them to the quilt. As in the photograph, sew the narrow and wide border fabrics together. Determine the placement of the checkerboards and measure the needed sections that will be attached to them. Attach the completed borders Log Cabin style, beginning on the right side, moving to the bottom, then continuing upward on the left side, making the top border the final addition.

Finish the quilt by adding batting and backing. Quilt and add the binding.

Design 8 Variations

The following diagrams show arrangements that can be sewn together in sections without any partial seams.

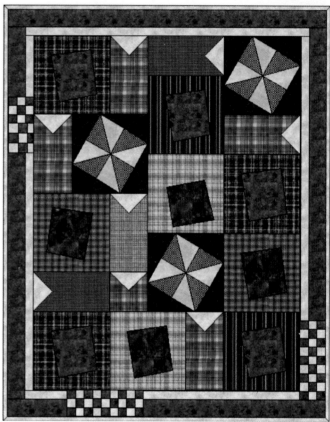

RIGHT: POCKETS, PLAID, AND PINWHEELS, detail. Full quilt on page 44.

Some Assembly Required • Margie Engel

We all have favorite blocks. Even if you have a long list of preferences, you might be interested in drawing some new ones. There is something invigorating about playing with block designs, so add that exercise to your portfolio as you design your quilts. For purposes of this book, I used some of my all-time favorites. You, the designer, must feel free to use them, change them, or ignore them!

The options for creating blocks from strip-sets are almost endless. You sew strips of fabrics together, then cut them apart and sew them back together again. Only a quilter would love such an activity! Equally fun, strip blocks can be rotated to create dynamic illusions that direct the viewer's eye, enhancing focal points and creating lines within the design.

Blocks such as these can be made to fit any space, another advantage that enables one to use different sized blocks within a quilt. For example, EYES ON THE SERENGETI contains 6" and 8" finished strip-set blocks.

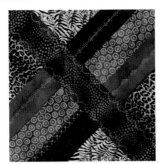

EYES ON THE SERENGETI, *detail, showing an 8" X Block and 6" quarter-square triangle block. 6" X Blocks are also used in this quilt.*

Strip-Set Blocks

Generally, for any given quilt I sew the strip-set blocks first and let the resulting block size dictate the size of additional blocks. This is so I do not have to be a mathematician! Having said that, should you want a specific block size, you can delight in square roots and triangles, or you can check each block's strip-set width in the ensuing directions! It is always wise to make a test block at the outset. To quickly check block measurements, draw the strip-set on graph paper, cut the segments, mark the quarter-inch seams, and tape the block together.

Strip-Set Sewing Tips

Strip-sets can be sewn using any number strips of any width. The strips are usually cut selvage to selvage. Sew the strips carefully, making sure to align the raw edges as you sew. Occasionally, strip-sets become wavy. To prevent this from happening, check the tension on your sewing machine before sewing. Correct tension should give you straight sets. Another preventative measure is to stitch each strip in the opposite direction of its predecessor.

There are some basic practices that facilitate making blocks from strip-sets. Because cutting strip-sets produces bias-edged block parts, you can give them added stability by spraying the uncut, sewn sets with starch or sizing. I lightly spray my block sets twice with fabric sizing, allowing them to air dry between applications. I like them to be very stiff, so sometimes I spray the sets a third time. Do not skip this—it is important.

After the strip-sets have dried, press them very well. Press them on the front, initially holding the fabric up so that the iron pushes the seams in the same direction. Turn the piece over and press again.

The strip-set blocks used in this book are cut at 45-degree angles. Look for the 45-degree line on your ruler and place a strip of masking tape alongside that line. This aids you in using the correct cut-

LEFT: EYES ON THE SERENGETI, detail. Full quilt on page 24.

Some Assembly Required • Margie Engel　　**51**

ting line since various angle lines are included on most rulers. Triangle-shaped rulers are also available.

I find that I get the most accurate cuts by using a smaller ruler (about 3" x 12") with the 45-degree angle line rather than cutting with a triangle, perhaps because I can hold down the longer ruler more securely.

After strip-set blocks are assembled, they need to be squared. The best method I have found is to use a square ruler that has a diagonal line through the middle. Place the diagonal line across the middle of the block so that trimming can be done on all sides of the block, maintaining its proportions. Various sizes of these rulers are readily available. I keep a 6½" and a 9½" square ruler close at hand for squaring filler blocks.

When sewing bias-edge blocks to straight-cuts, sew with the bias next to the machine's feed dogs when possible.

Strip-sets offer variety in block assemblage.

Focus fabrics used within strip-set blocks provide interest and continuity.

Strip-Set Block X

See this block in the quilts FINE FEATHERED FRIENDS (page 16), SPLASH (page 20), SOME ASSEMBLY REQUIRED (page 28), FUR & FLUFF (page 40), and FLOWER POWER (page 88).

Freezer Paper
Stability

In a hurry to sew but did not size/starch your fabric? Cut a strip of freezer paper equal to the size of the strip-set. Press the strip-set from the front, then turn it over and check that the seams are facing the desired direction. Place the freezer paper on the wrong side of the strip-set with the shiny side of the paper next to the fabric's wrong side. Press this well. Leave the paper intact throughout the cutting and sewing. The stability ensures straight blocks. Remove the freezer paper once the sewing is complete.

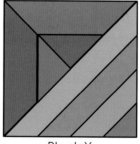

Block X

The "recipes" given for various sizes are for your convenience. You can easily create your own combinations.

Strip Cutting for Finished 5" Block

Strip-set 1 using 3 strips:
Cut 2 strips 1¾" wide.
Cut 1 strip 1½" wide.
The sewn strip-set is 4" wide.

Strip-set 2:
Cut 2 strips 1¾" wide.
The sewn strip-set is 3" wide.

Strip Cutting for Finished 6" Block

Strip-set 1 using 4 strips:
Strips B, C: Cut 2 strips 1½" wide.
Strips A, D: Cut 2 strips 1¾" wide.
The sewn strip-set is 5" wide.

Strip-set 2:
Strips E, F: Cut 2 strips 2¼" wide
The sewn strip-set is 4" wide.

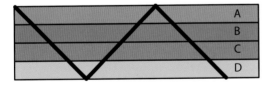

Cutting strip-set 1

45-degree cuts

Cutting strip-set 2

Cutting strip-sets for Block X

Strip Cutting for Finished 8" Block

Strip-set 1 using 5 strips:
Cut 2 strips 2" wide
Cut 3 strips 1½" wide
The sewn strip-set is 6½" wide.

Strip-set 2:
Cut 2 strips 2¾" wide.
The sewn strip-set is 5" wide.

Block X is assembled from 2 different strip-sets. In this example, one is made from 4 fabrics (top) and the other is made with 2 (bottom).

Cutting the Triangles

Place the strip-set on your cutting mat, lining up the 45-degree line on the ruler with a sewn seam or the edge of the strip-set. Make the first cut.

Angle the ruler in the opposite direction, align the 45-degree line to form a triangle, and cut.

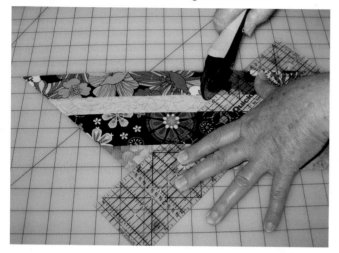

Continue cutting 45-degree triangles across the length of the strip-set.

The triangles cut from sets 1 and 2 differ in size. You'll need 2 triangles from strip-set 2 for every triangle cut from strip-set 1.

Cut twice as many strip-set 2 triangles as strip-set 1 triangles.

Sewing the Blocks

Arrange 1 strip-set 1 triangle and 2 strip-set 2 triangles as shown. When sewing the blocks, place the bias next to the machine's feed dogs to prevent the bias edge from stretching while being sewn.

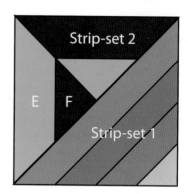

Sewing the strip-set 1 and strip-set 2 triangles

Align the strip-set 2 triangles right sides together and stitch. Press the seam to one side.

Place the strip-set 1 triangle atop the two-triangle unit, aligning the centers and points. Stitch. Press the seam open to facilitate joining the blocks later. Square the block to measure the desired size.

Strip-Set Block Y

See this block in the quilts FLORAL REFLECTIONS (page 19) and SPLASH (page 20).

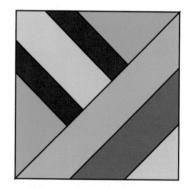

Block Y

Strip Cutting for Finished 4½ Block

Cut strips A, C, and E 2¼" wide.
Cut strips B and D 1½" wide.
The sewn strip-set is 7¾" wide.

Strip Cutting for Finished 5½" Block

Cut strips A and E 2¾" wide.
Cut strip C 2" wide.
Cut strips B and D 1½" wide.
The sewn strip-set is 8½" wide.

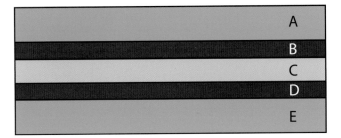

Block Y strip-set

If a finished 5" block is desired, use three 2¼" wide strips and two 1¾" strips. These comprise an 8¼" wide strip-set.

Cutting the Triangles

Use the width of the sewn strip-set to determine your cutting measurement. Cut the strip-set into squares, then divide the squares into quarters by cutting twice on the diagonal.

Steps to Cutting Block Y

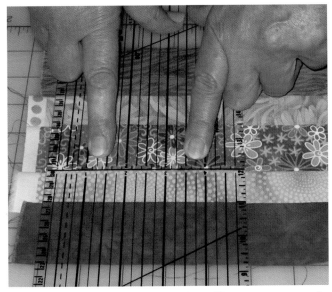

Align a straight line on the ruler with a sewn seam in the center of the strip-set.

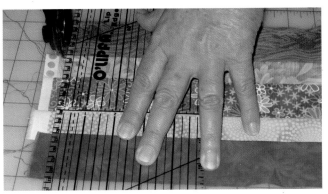

Keeping the ruler straight, straighten the edge of the strip-set.

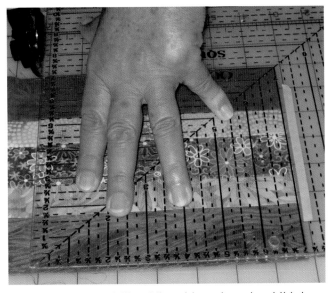

Measure the width of the strip-set and cut it into squares the size of the width. Using a square ruler facilitates accurate cutting. Note the masking tape placed alongside the 7" line, placed so that the correct line is easily spotted.

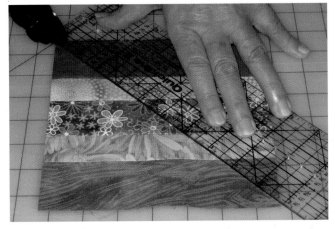

Place a ruler diagonally from corner to corner of a square and cut on the diagonal line. Carefully lift the ruler without moving the fabric.

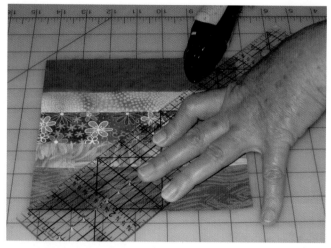

Carefully place the ruler diagonally along the opposite corners and make a second diagonal cut.

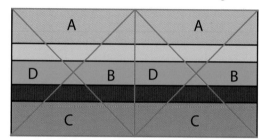

Label the sections as shown.

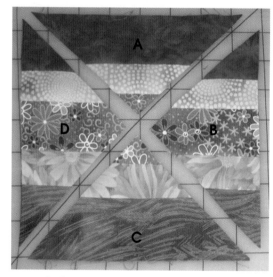

Cut and labeled Block Y triangles

Sewing the Blocks

Keeping the lettered sections consistent is important when arranging the blocks for sewing. Make half of the blocks by combining sections A & B and C & D. Make the other half by combining sections A & D and B & C. Sew the blocks by placing the section

with the straight grain facing upward and the piece with the bias edges next to the machine's feed dogs.

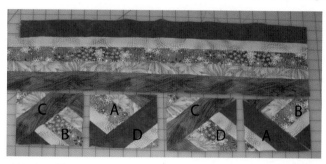

Work with pairs of blocks for consistent mirror images. For the first blocks, sew sections A & B together , then C & D (on the right). For the second blocks to mirror, sew sections A & D together, then B & C (on the left).

Strip-Set Block Z

See this block in Eyes on the Serengeti (page 24).

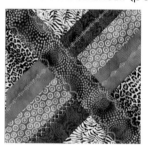

Block Z

Strip Cutting for Finished 6" Block

Cut 3 strips 1½" wide.

Cut 2 strips 3" wide.

The sewn strip-set is 8½" wide.

Cut the strip for the center of the block 1¾" wide.

Strip Cutting for Finished 8" Block

Cut 3 strips 2" wide.

Cut 2 strips 3½" wide.

The sewn strip-set is 11" wide.

Cut the strip for the center of the block 2¼" wide.

The triangles for this block are cut from strip-set squares, and 2 are joined together with a center strip to complete the block. These blocks align easily when assembling a quilt.

Cutting the Triangles

Follow the strip-set sewing, cutting, and labeling method used for Block Y (pages 54–56).

From each square, select the B and D triangles and join them with a center strip. Use the A and C triangles elsewhere in the quilt or in a border.

EYES ON THE SERENGETI, detail. The A and C triangles are used with the animal faces in the small blocks near the top of the quilt.

Sewing the Blocks

Place a B triangle right-side up and pin a separate fabric strip, right-side down, onto the base of the triangle (its longest edge). Sew with the triangle next to the feed dogs. Do not cut the center strip yet. Press the seam toward the center strip. Place the second triangle on the other side of the strip and align the triangles so that a well-matched square results. Sew with the triangle next to the feed dogs.

Press the block well and trim the excess from the center strip to yield a square.

Sew the middle strip to one triangle, right sides together. The strip must extend 1½" beyond the point of the triangle. Press the seam toward the center strip.

Align the bottom of the strip with the second triangle, aligning the triangle points and seams for a continuous visual line. Sew and press as before.

The completed Z block is ready to be squared.

Checkerboards from Strip-Sets

POCKETS, PLAIDS, AND PINWHEELS, detail

Cut 2 strips 1½" wide from each of 2 contrasting fabrics (4 total). Cut the strips in half.

Make a strip-set using one fabric as the center bordered by the second fabric on each side. Repeat this process, alternating the positions of the fabrics. You will have a half-strip of each fabric left over. Maintain ¼" seams so that the strip-sets measure 3½" wide.

Press the sets well. If they appear wavy, spray them with fabric sizing and allow it to dry before cutting the smaller sections.

To cut the sections, use a sewn seam as a reference point to align your ruler and cut 1" units from the strip-sets. Each set will yield 13–14 units. Alternate the units and join until the desired size is reached.

Pressing Thoughts

Good pressing determines the visual effect of checkerboards. The initial pressing is done when the long strips are joined into a strip-set. Press toward the darker strip, which yields seams that nudge into each other when the small units are sewn.

After the small units are sewn together into blocks or panels, consider pressing the seams open to produce an even appearance. The alternative, pressing to one side as initially done, results in the small units bulging on one side, presenting an uneven appearance and sometimes making machine quilting a challenge.

Quarter-Square Triangles

EYES ON THE SERENGETI, detail

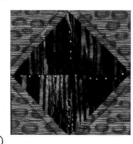

From 2 contrasting fabrics, cut a square 1¼" larger than your desired finished block size. (The blocks shown are 6" finished, so the initial squares were cut 7¼".)

On the wrong side of the lighter-colored square, draw a diagonal line from corner to corner. Place the marked square on the unmarked square, right sides together. Stitch ¼" from the marked line on both sides of the line. Cut on the marked line to yield 2 half-square triangle units. Press the seam allowance toward the darker fabric.

On the wrong side of one of the units, draw a diagonal line from corner to corner, with the line crossing both light and dark fabric. Place the 2 units right sides together, with contrasting fabrics facing each other. Stitch ¼" from each side of the drawn line, just as you did previously.

Cut on the drawn line to yield 2 quarter-square triangles. Press and square them to the unfinished size (in this example, 6½" x 6½").

Drunkard's Path

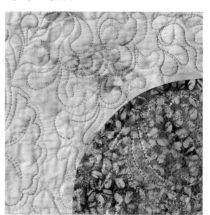

THIS NEW DAY, detail

Pin Point

Sometimes block parts need to be pinned and it is expedient to sew over the pins. To do this, use very thin straight pins and sew slowly.

Despite the curved seam, this block is relatively easy to sew. It does, however, require 3 thin pins (add more if you wish). Position one pin in the center and one at each end of the seam. I find it easiest to sew with the quarter circle on the top.

For a 6" finished block, trace the templates on page 87. Cut the 2 pieces from contrasting fabrics.

To sew the block, pin the centers of both curves right sides together. Then pin each side of the curves exactly as they are to be sewn. You may want to add pins between these places as well.

With the smaller unit facing up, sew the pieces slowly, matching the fabric edges as you go. This starts out feeling unwieldy, but quickly evens out and produces a lovely block as long as you make sure you take your time and use small (2.5mm) stitches to sew that all-important quarter-inch seam.

Acrylic
Templates

When I am making large numbers of this block, I use acrylic circle templates, finding the appropriately sized circle, and then drawing the square lines of the block onto the circle to use as reference lines. The 2 lines meet at the center of the circle template. I use markers that can be wiped off the acrylic with alcohol wipes. The acrylic circles allow me to cut the curves with a small (28mm) rotary cutter.

For a 6" finished block, I start with a 6½" square for the concave portion and a 4" square for the convex curve (the quarter circle).

Templates for Drunkard's Path are on page 87.

Pinwheel Block:
Envelope with Separate Flap

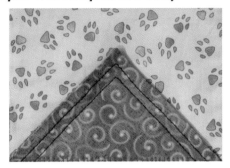

FUR & FLUFF, *detail*

For FUR & FLUFF, the Envelope block is 5" finished and is constructed from a strip-set. There is no seam line extending from the envelope flap because it is inserted into the seam. Flaps are similar to Prairie Points except they are thinner.

Constructing the Envelope Flaps

To construct 2 envelope flaps, cut 2 squares 4" x 4" from the same fabric. With right sides together and a 2mm stitch setting, sew a ¼" seam completely around the square.

Place a ruler diagonally on the square, from corner to corner, and cut it into 2 triangular pieces. Trim the points. Turn the pieces right-side out, push out the seams and points, and press.

The 2 squares yield 2 flaps.

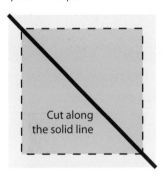

Cut along the solid line

Sewing squares for the envelope flaps

Poking
Pointer

An orangewood stick, which can be found among manicure supplies, comes in handy when pushing out points and corners of blocks. The stick has a flat end that smoothes and pushes out the seams when turning fabrics right-side out. It can also be used to "finger-press" seams. The pointed end serves as a useful and innocuous stiletto.

Constructing the Block

Cut 1 strip 2" wide and 1 strip 4" wide. Make a strip-set using ¼" seams. Press well. The sewn strip-set should measure 5½" wide. Cut 4 squares 5½" x 5½" from the strip-set.

Referring to the block photo, align the raw edges of a flap with the narrower strip in the square and baste the flap into position. Make 4.

Join 4 units to form a textured Pinwheel block.

Pinwheel block, Fur & Fluff, *detail*

Tab Inserts

Pockets, Plaids, and Pinwheels, *detail*

This method is for sewing Tab Inserts when using various fabrics and making one at a time. If you want tabs all of the same fabric, follow the preceding directions for the envelope flaps. Tabs can be inserted in any seam—within blocks, between blocks, within borders, or any other place your heart desires.

Fold a square in half, right sides together. At the fold line, mark the center. Drop down ¼" and from that point, draw a triangle, allowing for a ¼" seam beyond the line as shown.

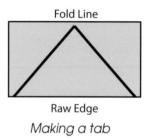

Making a tab

Stitch along the drawn lines and trim ¼" beyond the seam. Trim the point and turn right-side out. Press well. Position the tab onto its fabric base, aligning the raw edges. Baste in place.

For added interest, you can use 2 sizes of tabs inserted into the same seam.

This method enables you to make tabs from various fabrics with no duplicates.

9" Dancing Pinwheel Block

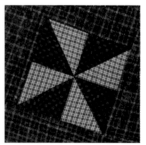

Pockets, Plaids, and Pinwheels, *detail*

Fast, easy, and fun to make from scraps, the Dancing Pinwheel tilts at any angle you choose. Because you add strips around the center pinwheel and trim them, you create a bias edge to the block. To stabilize these for sewing, it helps to spray the block with sizing before trimming. I sew all the blocks, then spray them and allow them to air dry while working on other parts of the quilt.

When sewing bias-edged blocks to other straight-edge blocks, pin the ends of the blocks together and stitch with the bias edge next to the machine's feed dogs.

Begin by making 4 half-square triangle units.

- Cut 2 squares 4" x 4" from each of 2 contrasting fabrics.

- Draw a diagonal line from corner to corner on the backs of the lighter squares.

- Place the contrasting squares right-sides together and stitch ¼" on both sides of the drawn line.

- Cut on the drawn line and press the half-square triangle units open.

- Square up the units to measure 3½" x 3½".

Sew the half-square triangle units into a pinwheel unit. Press the seams open after sewing the pairs of half-square triangles together to simplify the final stitching.

Add a 3½" strip around the pinwheel unit, Log Cabin style, stitching one side at a time. Press the seams toward the strip and trim it even with the pinwheel unit after each addition.

Spray the block with sizing and allow it to air dry.

With the block atop a cutting mat, place a 9½" square ruler on the block and turn it so that the inside pinwheel is tilted within the square. No particular angle is required; just turn the ruler until you like the way the block tilts. Carefully trim all 4 sides.

Trimming the Dancing Pinwheel block

If you don't have a 9½" square ruler, use a larger ruler and mark the lines at 9½" with tape to help keep your eyes on the correct measurement.

Frame Block

This simple block provides a wonderful framework for larger elements. Its usefulness is evident in the ELECTRIC MOLAS quilt in the gallery (page 90).

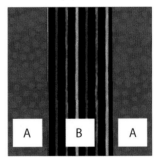

Frame block

Constructing the Block

For a 5" finished block, cut:

2 strips of a solid fabric 2" wide (A).
1 strip of a striped fabric 2½" wide (B).

Join the strips in a strip-set as shown. The sewn strip-set should measure 5½" wide.

Cut squares 5½" x 5½". If you cut the strips selvage to selvage, the strip-set should yield 7 Frame blocks.

Ah, the wonderful world of embellishments—where anything is possible and limited only by how a particular item can be attached to a project. Today, we do not ask what quilters will add to their quilts. Instead, we wonder what they will not add!

The quilter who tiptoes into embellishing often begins with thread enhancements. There are numerous delicious threads from which to choose. Just be sure to use the appropriate needle. Thread embellishing by hand can generally be achieved with embroidery needles.

For thread embellishing by machine, there are several needle types to choose from. Use metallic or topstitch needles for metallic threads, and sharps needles, rather than universal, for other threads. Adapt the needle size to the thread size. Lower numbered threads are thicker, so they need higher numbered needles (go figure!). It is best when the hole created by the needle is filled with the thread. I generally use a 70/10 or 80/12 size needle for most thread projects. Rarely do I have to move up to a size 90/14. If I intend to switch between metallic threads and other fibers, I use a topstitch needle so that I am not constantly changing needles.

Do not overlook the fact that if a thread is too thick for a needle, you can wind it on your bobbin and stitch bottom-side up. Mention bobbin thread embellishing, and some people's eyes widen as their brains say, "Oh my." Others jump at the choice and discover that it is very easy after they have figured out how to indicate where to stitch. Often, preliminary stitching on the top establishes those guides.

Buttons and beads are among the foremost embellishments. They can be sewn by hand or machine, but most bead enthusiasts stitch their beads by hand. It becomes an emotional bonding experience! You need to know that hand beading needles ex-

ist—some very long and thin for small beads, others shorter and heavier for penetrating several layers of fabrics. Embroidery needles also work efficiently.

SOME ASSEMBLY REQUIRED, detail.
Buttons can be used anywhere and everywhere as long as they are securely fastened.

Long-term beaders will tell you to use beading thread, which is available in bead and craft shops. The primary requirement is that the thread be strong with little elasticity, yet still thin enough to pass through the bead along with the needle. Thread color also plays a role since it shows through some beads.

Zillions of heart-stopping beads are on the market! Fabriholics who become thread fanatics can easily become bead enthusiasts. Why not? All it takes is more drawer space! Be aware that some beads will fade in bright light; others can withstand washing but not dry cleaning; bugle beads have such a sharp edge that they need to be attached with seed beads at the ends to prevent cutting the thread. The common seed bead is available in a vast array of colors and you can find plenty of same-sized beads. Like everything, quality beads will cost slightly more than basic craft beads. If you are going to put your valuable time into sewing them to your quilts, you probably want better quality.

Some adventurous folks even make their own beads! The basic materials can be clay, glass, plastic, metal, or fabric. If you want to try a new pastime, find a book and get started.

When and how to bead is an individual decision. Because I want my beads anchored very well, I sew them onto completed projects that have been quilted. This way, I can guide the needle through the batting for stability, bringing the needle up before it penetrates the quilt back. Generally, I do not bead before machine quilting because the beads could create quilting problems. Hand quilters have the option of beading whenever they choose.

JACOBEAN HOLIDAY, detail. Embroideries such as these Jacobean florals provide beautiful areas for beads.

When the moment comes that you want to add something "odd" to your quilt do not hesitate. You do not have to get permission, but you do have to figure out how to attach it. Personally, I draw the line at gluing objects to my quilts, so I have to bore holes (as in seashells), or add tulle and stitch the tulle down with monofilament to keep the item in place. Select dark rather than light-colored tulle. Lighter colors reflect light differently and can obscure the item you want to showcase.

Surface embellishment also includes using paints, dyes, inks, and foils. It is no longer unusual to see quilts incorporating some or all of these media. Beautiful books on this subject are available. The topic stirs the hearts of many and throws up a curtain to others who automatically say, "I'm not an artist; I can't do that."

Listen up. Yes you can! If you fear adding this sort of embellishment to your fabric, begin with colored pencils. It is a return to childhood. If holding a paintbrush inhibits you, look into oil sticks, which resemble fat crayons. Later, you can buy a paintbrush and thrill over inks and paints. Take a class or buy the book that makes you drool and try the techniques. So much fun awaits you!

Look at the pictures below. They show all-purpose inks applied to enhance fabric design in the quilt FLORAL REFLECTIONS from Design 1 (page 19). The ink is used to unify the flower theme by adding floral shapes to existing circles within the fabric. I applied the ink with ink daubers, sponge "sticks" that absorb the ink and are then used like a fabric marker.

This is the original fabric for FLORAL REFLECTIONS.

Here is the fabric with applied ink, used to create flower-like shapes.

When your experiments lead you to fabric paints, eyeball AUGUST MOON (page 66) with its moonlit water and stars, sparkling because of pearlescent paint. The turtles and seashells are also painted.

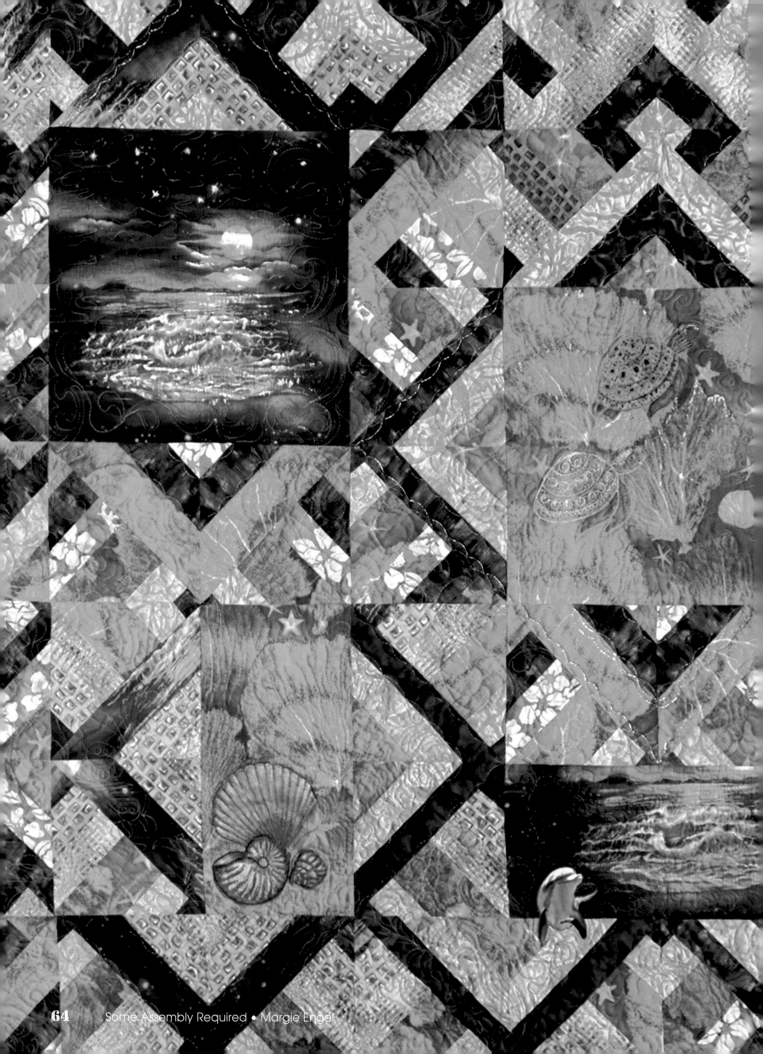

Some Assembly Required • Margie Engel

The excitement begins as a new quilt idea takes priority in our brains. It sparkles and dances and gives great promise. Out come the fabrics and our creative juices are ignited.

The Design Process

Hopefully, you have a design wall. By placing pieces and parts on the wall, you can scrutinize them vertically and at a distance. You can change something, walk away, come back, ask "What if…," and take a digital photo for reference. Remember, quilts look different when you stand several feet away from them.

This trial-and-error becomes a natural process and feeds artistic development. However, what happens when you repeatedly try out possibilities and make changes only to discover that the quilt that began with an exciting idea just is not coming together? What do you do then?

Quit? Put the pieces away for a while? Don't laugh—at this point sometimes it is better to put the quilt to rest for a while rather than to continue adding frustration. Maybe you will come back to it, maybe not. Perhaps you have learned enough from that project. You have not wasted time or fabric— you've learned and progressed. Sometimes learning what does not work is as valuable as producing a finished product.

You could call in your critique buddy, the creative person who enjoys sharing quilts in process and makes honest observations. A friend like this is priceless, especially when both of you have learned to evaluate without taking observations personally. We all know that it is hard to be objective when feeling emotional about a quilt or an element within the quilt.

At the end of the day, you might turn to a mental checklist, asking the following questions:
- Does the mood "speak" as hoped?
- Does everything appear to belong, giving a feeling of unity?
- Does the design give a feeling of balance?
- Is there enough contrast in values?
- Would an additional change in color temperature help?
- Is there a focal point?
- Does your eye have a place to rest?
- Do the lines created by color successfully move the eye?
- Is there variety in size and placement to add spice?

While you are questioning, be aware that sometimes the true problem is sitting alongside an element that you think is the offending culprit. If color is the issue, try placing a different value or hue over various pieces. Often I see students produce a beautiful central area in a quilt and then arbitrarily add a sash or border without auditioning optional hues or values for the sash.

Sashes and borders should complement the piece they surround without claiming all the attention. A poor choice of sashing fabric can take over a quilt. This problem is easy to avoid or amend simply by auditioning fabrics. When doing this, remember to audition the same amount that will be in the quilt by placing it under the adjoining fabrics on the design wall.

One more exercise deserves consideration. Occasionally, a quilt can benefit from being cut apart and rearranged. Gasp now and reach for the camera instead of the rotary cutter. It is great fun to print a few copies on paper and then cut them apart and rearrange the pieces. I have used this trick to retrieve lost causes and turn them into award winners!

LEFT: August Moon, detail. Full quilt on page 66.

Lessons from the Design Wall

Here is an example of a res-cued quilt. AUGUST MOON was to have been a memoir of a night launch of a NASA satellite—an incredible sight and a quilt with emotional ties. My idea was to produce an ocean scene and finish it with a quilting pattern of the shuttle. Here are the salient issues that arose.

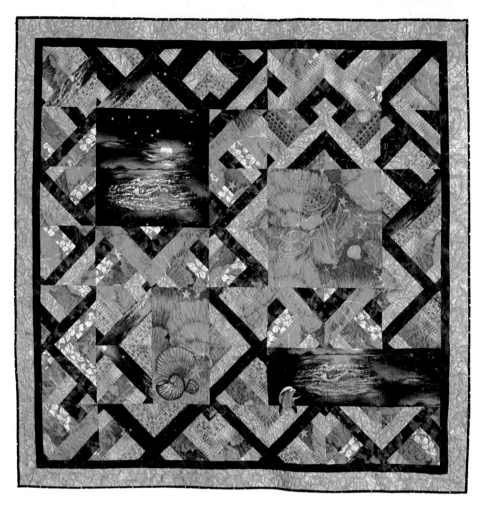

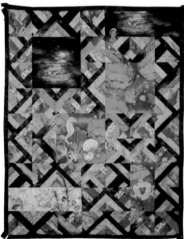

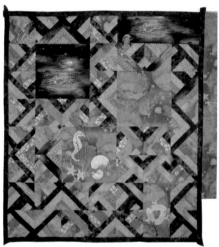

With the proposed quilt on the wall, I could see that the light blue horizontal strip, a painted panel of seashells near the bottom, was totally out of place. The light value claimed too much attention and did not fit with the other elements. The immediate answer was to omit the questionable block or to paint it a darker value. Had I looked carefully at this point, I would have seen the possibility of two quilts!

Here is still another possibility. The shells will have to be darkened. What if another underwater fabric block were inserted at the bottom? Better still, perhaps the dark horizontal fabric on the top right should be moved nearer to the bottom of the quilt.

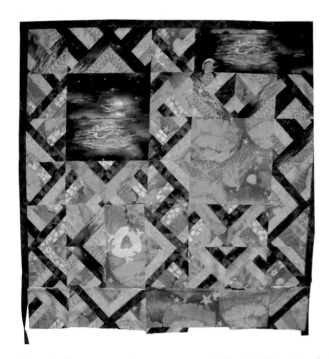

Here is the second arrangement. The light horizontal block is gone. Ooops! I wanted the moon/ocean block at the top to be the focal point, but in this version, my eye is pulled to the fish because of the extremely different value.

The quilt is better, but there is still a lack of balance. The idea to move the top right fabric panel is gaining favor. I think it is worth a try.

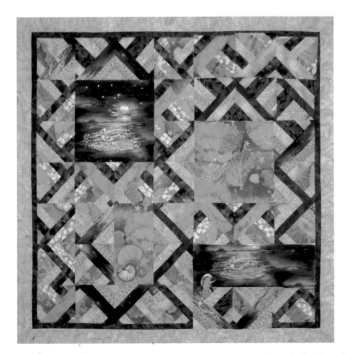

Some days you just have to make a decision! Finished is better than perfect, so I think the quilt top will be sewn in this arrangement. Effective quilting will help it immensely. Where is the shuttle launch? In my memory, awaiting a better quilt.

AUGUST MOON is off the wall and here are the leftovers for another day. "What if..." another quilt idea presents itself?

Some Assembly Required • Margie Engel   **67**

Appliqué is a definitive type of embellishment and a delightful addition to quilts. Literally, an appliqué is fabric applied to another fabric. There are numerous ways to do this and many books that elaborate on various techniques.

One of my favorite methods uses fusible interfacing and colored pencils and is well explained in my book *Bodacious Appliqué à la Carte*, which provides a good read and delightful patterns (according to my friends!). It is the method I used for the appliquéd flowers in Jacobean Holiday and for the birds in Fine Feathered Friends.

Jacobean Holiday, appliqué detail

Fine Feathered Friends, appliqué detail

Another choice method harkens back to our ancestors—broderie perse. Motifs are cut from fabrics, historically floral chintzes, and stitched to another fabric. This is an effective way to use some of those gorgeous motifs found in fabrics. One example of this method features some of the fish applied to Splash.

Splash, broderie perse appliqué detail

There are times when I think the motif would stand out a little better if it had an outline. A great solution is to fuse the design to felt, suede, or any fabric that is sturdy and does not ravel. I can apply the motif to felt and then have the choice of cutting the felt into graphic shapes or following the motif shape with an extended border.

Another type of appliqué used in this book begins with digitized machine embroidery designs. Some folks bravely hoop their quilt tops to add machine embroidery. Since I am a fanatic about puckers, I use the embroidery designs as appliqués. There are two methods that work well for me. The first is simple. The embroidery is done on the fabric of choice, which is then applied to the quilt top. An example of this is in Eyes on the Serengeti. In the center bottom block, appliqués are embroidered rectangles—the tiger on felt and the zebra on printed cotton, which is purposely fringed.

Eyes on the Serengeti, machine embroidery appliqué detail

Another example of digitized machine embroidery is shown in Some Assembly Required. The machine embroidery is stitched on felt, then trimmed, leaving the felt border. The appliqué stitches are easily secured through the felt.

Some Assembly Required, machine embroidery appliqué detail

The applied embroidery method takes a little more work, but gives me freedom in placement. I embroider the design on organdy or organza placed on top of two layers of tulle. Some tulles have a great deal of elasticity, so I place the grain of the tulle pieces in opposite directions to minimize the stretch. With the three layers hooped, I embroider the motif.

Next, I cut out the motif as close as possible to the stitching and finish the edge by running a heated electric stencil cutter around it. The heat melts the synthetic organza and tulle, resulting in a finished edge. It also seals the edges of the thread when I use polyester. By using polyester thread, I do not have to be concerned about whether or not the digitizing provides a border stitch line (and many designs do not).

For an example of this method, look at the black-and-white flowers on SOME ASSEMBLY REQUIRED.

SOME ASSEMBLY REQUIRED, detail. Digitized machine embroidered flowers are stitched onto layers of tulle and organza and appliquéd to the quilt.

Often, life is best when it is kept simple, a liberating theory that applies when creating appliqués with paper-backed fusible web. Because it is repositionable, Steam-a-Seam 2® fusible web (regular or lite) made my life very easy when producing the critters for the POCKETS, PLAIDS AND PINWHEELS quilt. If you opt to use fusible web be sure you follow the manufacturer's instructions. Also, remember that when drawing a design on the paper backing you need a mirror image; reverse the design so that it finishes in the desired direction.

Appliqué Patterns

Use the following appliqué patterns to suit your fancy and your quilts. Remember, it's your quilt, so change them, resize them, or replace them at your whim. Not only can you design quilts, you can also draw if you give yourself the chance.

- Three birds for FINE FEATHERED FRIENDS (pages 71–74).

- Two floral blocks for JACOBEAN HOLIDAY, including one large flower, two leaves, and half of the lower panel, which is to be flipped and mirrored for the other half of the panel (pages 75–77).

- Trapunto design, two sizes of daisies, and a ginkgo leaf quilting design for THIS NEW DAY (pages 78–81).

- Four pages of critters used on nine blocks on POCKETS, PLAIDS & PINWHEELS (pages 82–86).

FINE FEATHERED FRIENDS

These are one-fabric appliqués that are highlighted with Prismacolor® Premier Colored Pencils . This raw-edged method relies on applying fusible interfacing to the back of the appliqué before it is embellished and added to the background (see Resources, page 94).

The appliqués are machine sewn to the background fabric, usually with a blanket stitch using matching and variegated threads and a sharp needle.

Parakeet appliqué

Parrot appliqué

THIS NEW DAY

Trapunto design

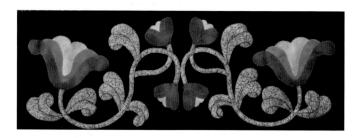

Tropical Red Bird appliqué

Appliquéd daisy

JACOBEAN HOLIDAY

The floral appliqués are sewn using the same method referred to above in FINE FEATHERED FRIENDS. Use the Bodacious method or your own favorite technique.

POCKETS, PLAIDS, AND PINWHEELS

All of the pocket critters are fused with Steam-a-Seam 2 and directly applied to the background fabrics. In some cases, they overlap blocks and are sewn down after the block portions are assembled. They are embellished with Prismacolor pencils and stitching. I used a blanket stitch, various colored threads, and sharp needles.

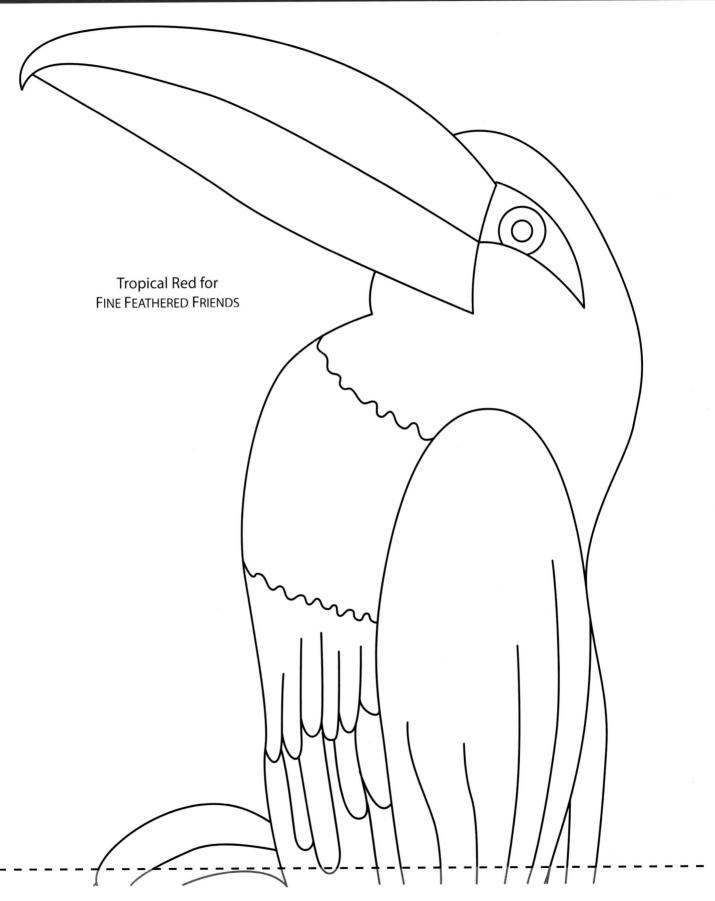

Tropical Red for
FINE FEATHERED FRIENDS

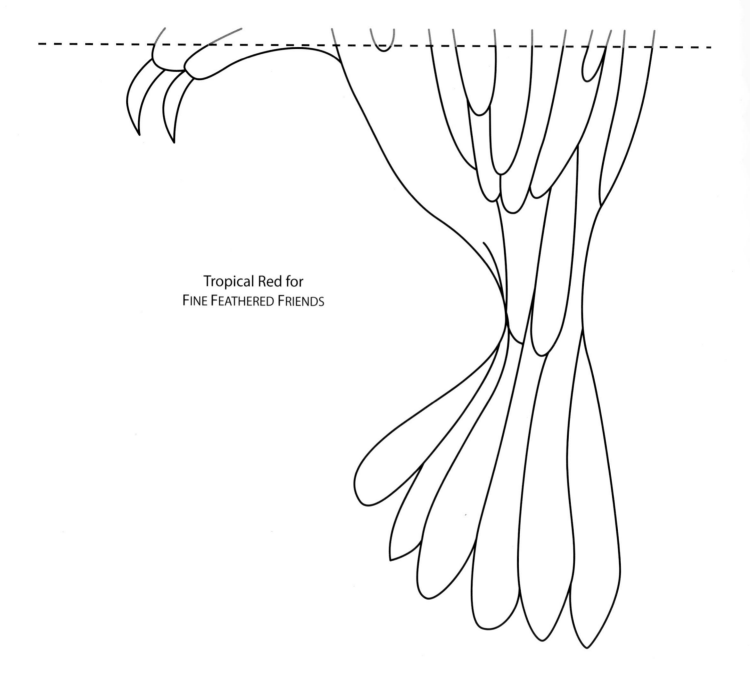

Tropical Red for
FINE FEATHERED FRIENDS

Parrot for
FINE FEATHERED FRIENDS

Parakeet for
FINE FEATHERED FRIENDS

½ of bottom panel

Top →

Appliqué pattern for
bottom panel in
Jacobean Holiday

Make a mirror image
of this design for the left side
of the bottom floral panel.

Appliqué flower pattern
for center block in
JACOBEAN HOLIDAY

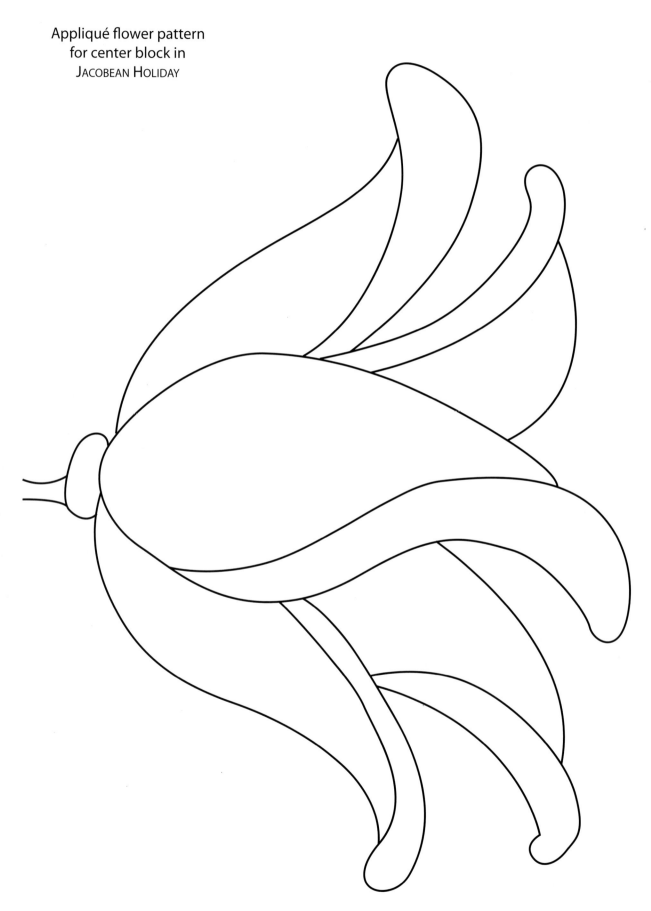

Appliqué patterns for
leaves in JACOBEAN HOLIDAY

Top ↑

Top ↑

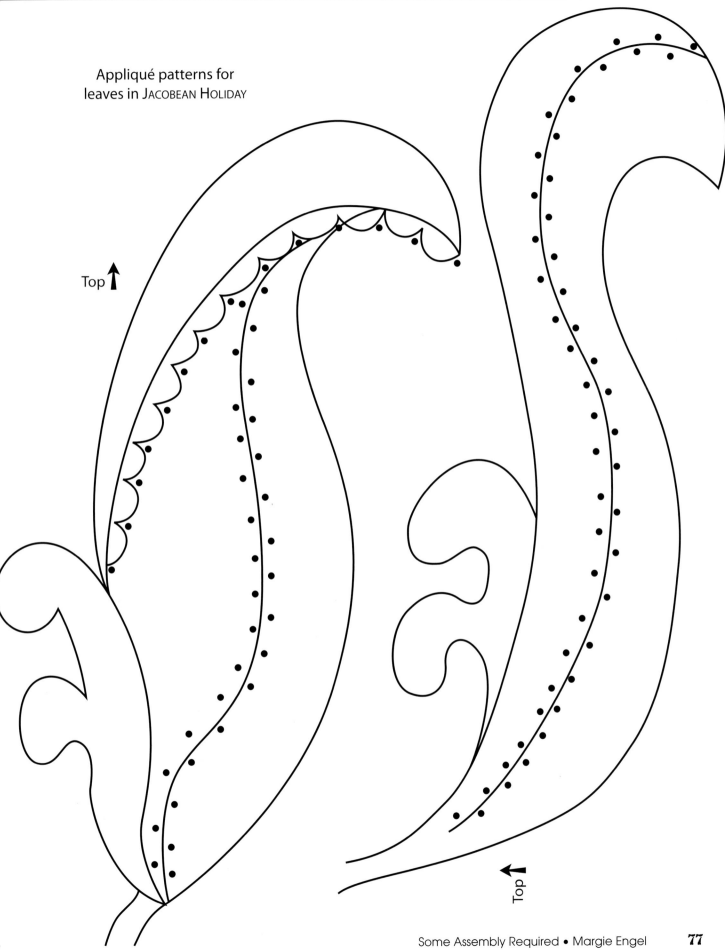

Ginkgo Leaf quilting design

Daisies for THIS NEW DAY

Match to bottom of Top Section

Trapunto Design
Middle Section
for THIS NEW DAY

Match to top of
Lower Section

Match to bottom
of Center Section

Trapunto Design
Lower Section
for THIS NEW DAY

Trapunto Design
Upper Section
for THIS NEW DAY

Match to top of Center Section

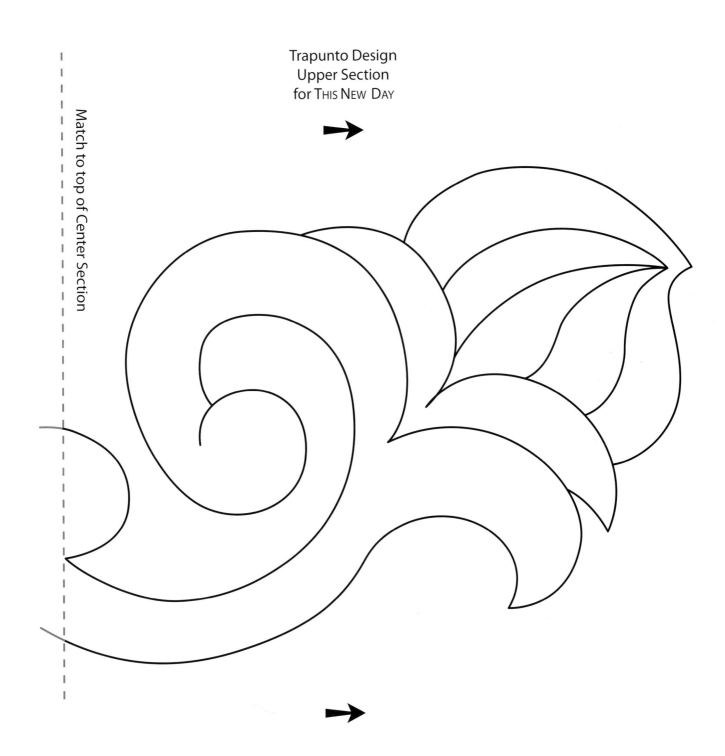

Appliqué designs for
POCKETS, PLAIDS, AND PINWHEELS

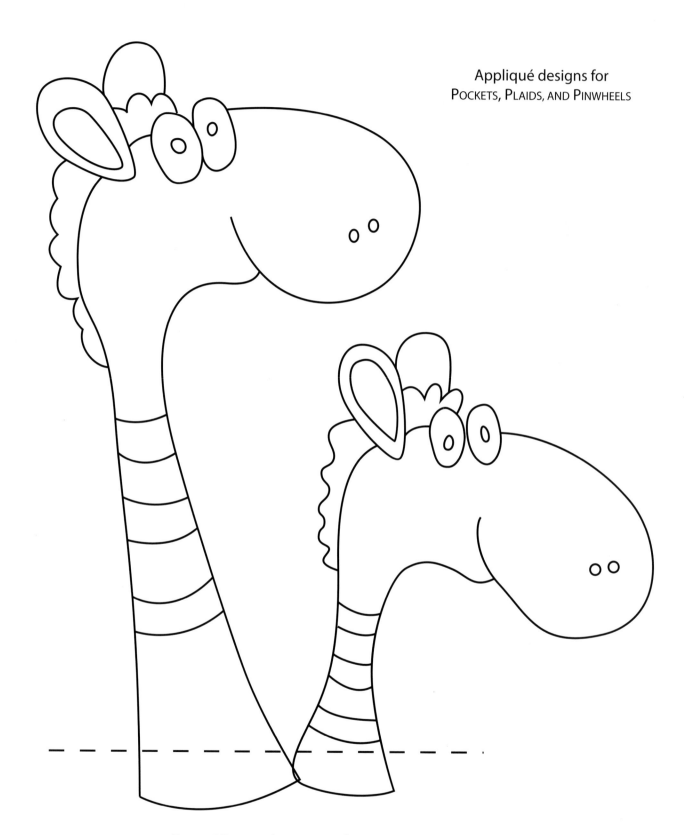

Dotted lines indicate top of pocket

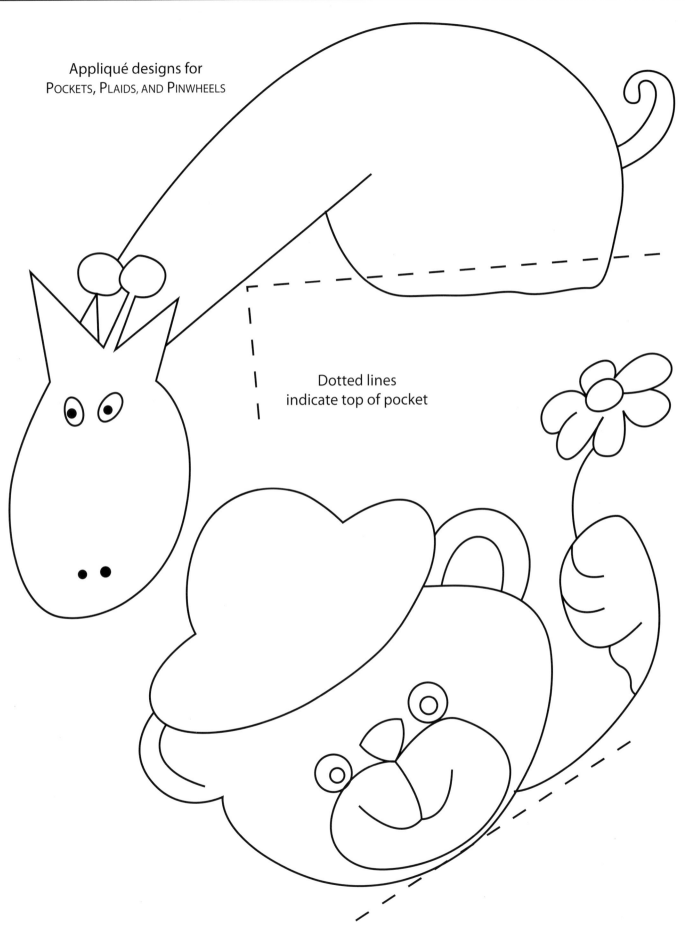

Appliqué designs for
POCKETS, PLAIDS, AND PINWHEELS

Dotted lines
indicate top of pocket

Appliqué designs for
POCKETS, PLAIDS, AND PINWHEELS

Dotted lines
indicate top of pocket

Appliqué designs for
POCKETS, PLAIDS, AND PINWHEELS

Dotted lines indicate top of pocket

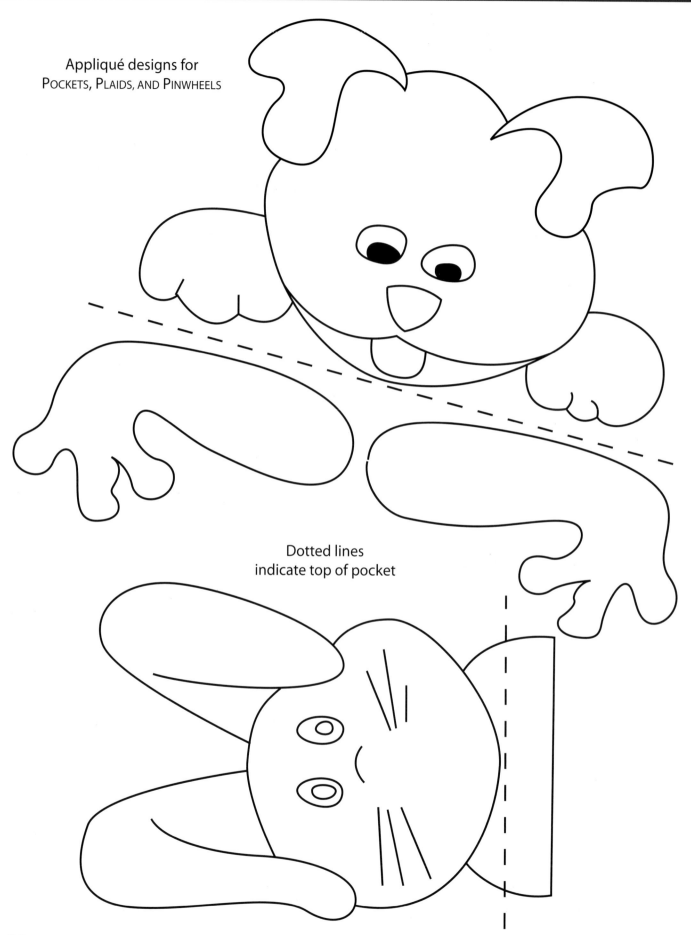

Appliqué designs for
POCKETS, PLAIDS, AND PINWHEELS

Dotted lines
indicate top of pocket

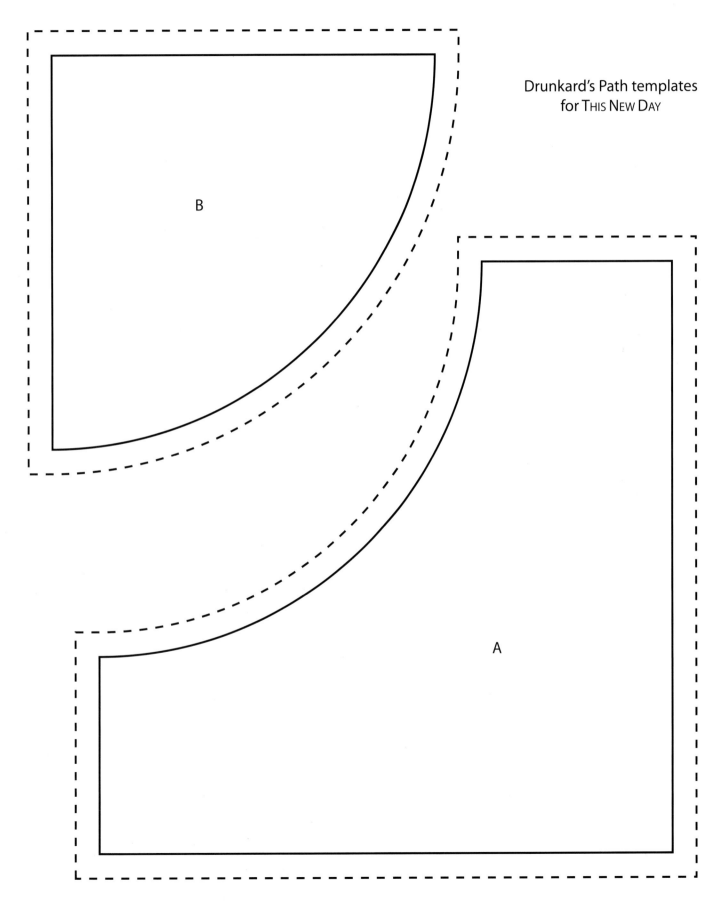

Drunkard's Path templates
for THIS NEW DAY

B

A

INSPIRATION! AN IDEA GALLERY

All the gallery quilts were made and quilted by the author. Gallery photos by John Engel.

FLOWER POWER, 36" x 49"

FLOWER POWER is related to SOME ASSEMBLY REQUIRED. It consists of twenty-four 6½"
x 6½" blocks. The blocks follow a symmetrical rotation pattern. The appliquéd flowers are cut from one of the fabrics used in the quilt.

PANAMANIAN TREASURES, 41" x 37"

If your heart flutters over the amazing needlework achieved by the Panamanian and San Blas women who produce molas, you no longer have to travel
to distant locations to secure them. They are as close as your computer and
the Internet! Of course, if you use the Internet you will not have the stories of
searching for just the right ones, so go ahead and book a cruise now!

Meanwhile, at home you can use the symmetrical Design 5 (page 32) and ex-
change molas for the embroideries, or you can opt for asymmetrical explora-
tions such as in this quilt.

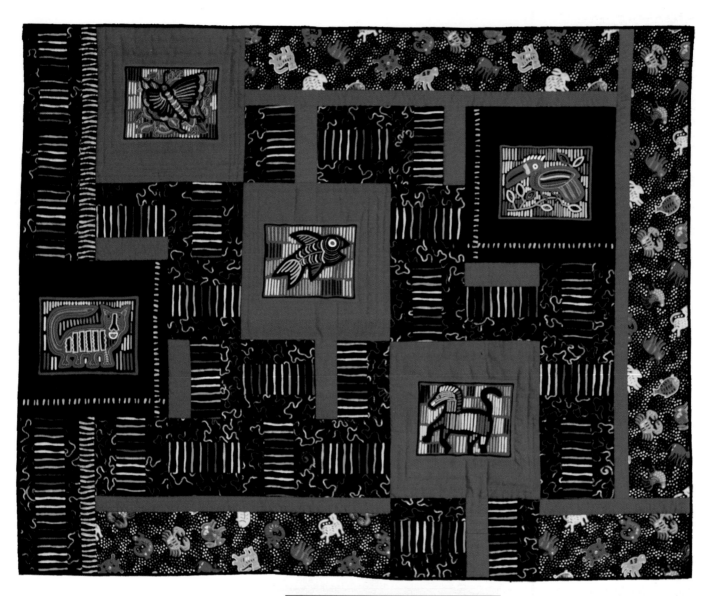

ELECTRIC MOLAS, 44" x 35"
More fun with molas! Still with rapid heartbeats over molas, I was excited to find these machine embroidered versions of molas, Molas Nouveau 5 x 7, created by Laura Waterfield of Laura's Sewing Studio (see Resources, page 94). The filler blocks, frequent additions to my simple quilts, are included in the block chapter (pages 50–61).

POCKET ORGANIZER, 11" x 27"
Recycling jeans pockets has been a recurring theme for my children's sewing camps. One favorite project is a jeans pocket organizer that, for a student, holds pencils and rulers and markers. For a quilter, the pockets offer safe storage for rotary cutters as well as markers and scissors. Look closely and you will see it is also a resting place for quilt show pins. This project is a forerunner to my pocket quilts.

RABBITVILLE, 42" x 34"

It is not just the pockets that recycle well. Here is a quilt that combines preprinted panels and the rest of the jeans. The seams on the jeans legs were just too tempting and had to be used as well. Jeans seams present their own challenges! I push batting into the bottom of the pockets to provide padding where scissors are stored.

SPRINGTIME, 44" x 50"

SPRINGTIME is the product of a class exercise. I pre-sewed the strip-sets and took them to students who played with various block arrangements and decided on this arrangement. Note the change in fabrics in the side blocks that offers the appearance of a trellis. The intention is to use the quilt as a backdrop for appliqué.

WHERE? RESOURCES

Remember to support your local quilt shop.
Ask if they carry the product you are seeking. They may be happy to order it for you.
The following lists the products used in the quilts in this book that work well for me.

BOOK

Bodacious Applique à la Carte by Margie Engel,
(AQS, 2008), www.engelquilts.com

COMPUTER SOFTWARE AND PRINTABLE FABRICS

The Electric Quilt and a variety of inkjet printable
fabrics, The Electric Quilt Company,
www.electricquilt.com

EMBROIDERY DESIGNS

Molas Nouveau 5 x 7 by Laura Waterfield,
www.LaurasSewingStudio.com

Animal Instincts and Crewel Embroidery by Iris Lee,
Oklahoma Embroidery Supply and Design
www.embroideryonline.com,
also sold by BERNINA dealers

Funky Flowers by Margit Grimm (Embroidery 125),
Husqvarna Viking,
www.myembroideries.com,
also sold by Husqvarna Viking dealers

INTERFACING

100% cotton smooth fusible interfacing for
appliques, HTC Form-Flex®, available through
quilt shops and www.engelquilts.com

EMBELLISHMENT SUPPLIES

Prismacolor® Premier Softcore colored pencils
www.prismacolor.com

Pigma® Micron® pens and brushes
www.sakuraofamerica.com

Tsukineko® all purpose inks and Fabrico® markers
www.tsukineko.com

Shiva®Paintstiks and numerous embellishments,
Embellishment Village
www.embellishmentvillage.com

Shiva®Paintstiks
www.cedarcanyontextiles.com

PAPER-BACKED FUSIBLE WEB AND BATTING

Steam-a-Seam 2® paper-backed fusible and
Warm 'n Natural® Batting, The Warm Company,
www.warmcompany.com

THREADS

Large variety of wonderful threads,
www.superiorthreads.com

Beautiful threads and silk ribbons,
www.ylicorp.com

Isacord embroidery threads sold by
BERNINA dealers, www.amannusa.com

LIVING BODACIOUSLY!
ABOUT THE AUTHOR

"I live in Paradise," says Margie Engel, a Florida beach resident. It is bodacious living at its best, with dolphins playing in the back "yard," orchids blooming on the deck, and a studio teeming with fabrics and threads. There are also boxes bulging with quilt show ribbons, including multiple Best of Show and Judge's Choice awards (including SOME ASSEMBLY REQUIRED!). Her favorite blue ribbons are for BODACIOUS BEAUREGARD, the parrot on the cover of her book *Bodacious Appliqué à la Carte* (AQS, 2008).

This active quilter/author credits her husband, John, for keeping life interesting even after 43 years of marriage. John is photographer, advisor, and computer guru for Margie's quilting activities—the reason she gains added time to accomplish a variety of endeavors.

This International Professional Quilters Association's 2009 Teacher of the Year has also received many awards for teaching abilities and for service. Margie was given the Jefferson Award for Public Service and the Brevard County Medal of Excellence, accolades presented her for the development and continuity of EduQuilters, an educational group she founded to teach quiltmaking to children in schools, organizations, and summer camps.

Dreaming up innovative events is another of Margie's strong points. She holds quilt workshops for high school sewing teachers on land, leads retreats aboard cruise ships, creates special events for quilt guilds, and holds annual "quilt escapes" in Kentucky and Florida. Margie may not be home often, but you can reach her through her website, www.engelquilts.com.

MORE AQS BOOKS

This is only a small selection of the books available from the American Quilter's Society. AQS books are known worldwide for timely topics, clear writing, beautiful color photos, and accurate illustrations and patterns. The following books are available from your local bookseller, quilt shop, or public library.

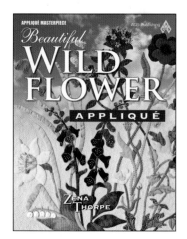

#8526

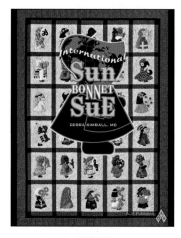

#8347

#8351

#8355

#8530

#7769

#8242

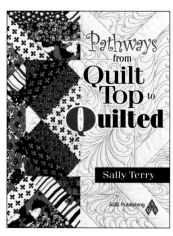

#8348

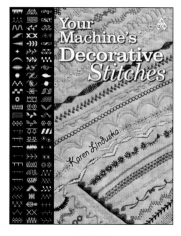

#8353

LOOK for these books nationally.
CALL or **VISIT** our website at

1-800-626-5420
www.AmericanQuilter.com